CAMPAIGN 321

TENOCHTITLAN 1519–21

Clash of Civilizations

SI SHEPPARD

ILLUSTRATED BY PETER DENNIS
Series editor Marcus Cowper

OSPREY PUBLISHING
Bloomsbury Publishing Plc

Kemp House, Chawley Park, Cumnor Hill, Oxford OX2 9PH, UK
29 Earlsfort Terrace, Dublin 2, Ireland
1385 Broadway, 5th Floor, New York, NY 10018, USA
Email: info@ospreypublishing.com
www.ospreypublishing.com

OSPREY is a trademark of Osprey Publishing Ltd

First published in Great Britain in 2018

A catalogue record for this book is available from the British Library.

Print ISBN: 978 1 4728 2018 1
ePDF: 978 1 4728 2020 4
eBook: 978 1 4728 2019 8
XML: 978 1 4728 2696 1

Maps by www.bounford.com
3D BEVs by The Black Spot
Index by Zoe Ross
Typeset by PDQ Digital Media Solutions, Bungay, UK
Printed and bound in India by Replika Press Private Ltd.

22 23 24 25 26   10 9 8 7 6 5 4

Artist's note
Readers may care to note that the original paintings from which
the colour plates in this book were prepared are available for private
sale. All reproduction copyright whatsoever is retained by the publishers.
All enquiries should be addressed to:

Peter Dennis
Fieldhead, The Park
MANSFIELD
Notts, NG18 2AT, UK

Email: magie.h@ntlworld.com

The publishers regret that they can enter into no correspondence upon
this matter.

The Woodland Trust
Osprey Publishing supports the Woodland Trust, the UK's leading
woodland conservation charity.

www.ospreypublishing.com
To find out more about our authors and books visit our website. Here you
will find extracts, author interviews, details of forthcoming events and
the option to sign-up for our newsletter.

Dedication

To my son, Zachary,
Who lives in an Age of Empires

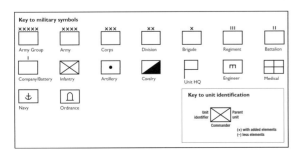

CONTENTS

The global strategic situation, 1492

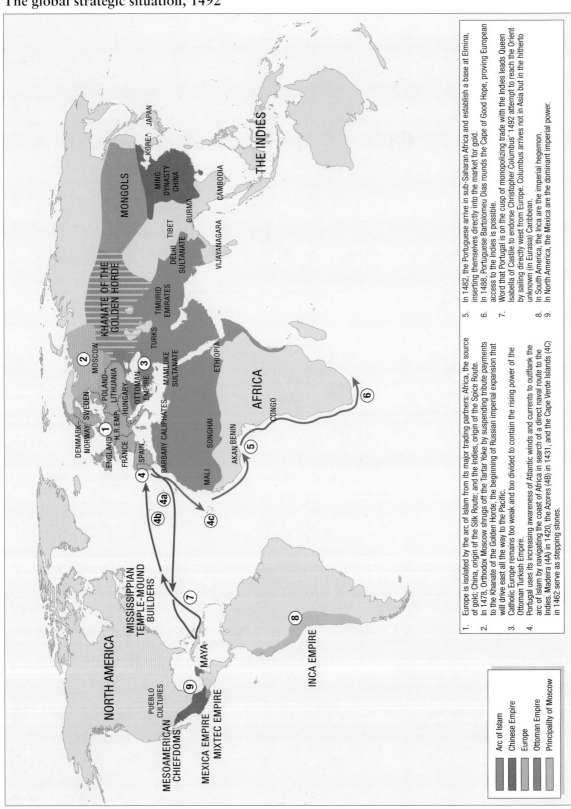

1. Europe is isolated by the the arc of Islam from its major trading partners: Africa, the source of gold; China, origin of the Silk Route; and the Indies, origin of the Spice Route.

2. In 1478, Orthodox Moscow shrugs off the Tartar Yoke by suspending tribute payments to the Khanate of the Golden Horde, the beginning of Russian imperial expansion that will drive east all the way to the Pacific.

3. Catholic Europe remains too weak and too divided to contain the rising power of the Ottoman Turkish Empire.

4. Portugal uses its increasing awareness of Atlantic winds and currents to outflank the arc of Islam by navigating the coast of Africa in search of a direct naval route to the Indies. Madeira (4A) in 1420, the Azores (4B) in 1431, and the Cape Verde Islands (4C) in 1462 serve as stepping stones.

5. In 1482, the Portuguese arrive in sub-Saharan Africa and establish a base at Elmina, inserting themselves directly into the market for gold.

6. In 1488, Portuguese Bartolomeu Dias rounds the Cape of Good Hope, proving European access to the Indies is possible.

7. Word that Portugal is on the cusp of monopolizing trade with the Indies leads Queen Isabella of Castile to endorse Christopher Columbus' 1492 attempt to reach the Orient by sailing directly west from Europe. Columbus arrives not in Asia but in the hitherto unknown (in Eurasia) Caribbean.

8. In South America, the Inca are the imperial hegemon.

9. In North America, the Mexica are the dominant imperial power.

ORIGINS OF THE CAMPAIGN

'No one would have believed,' wrote H. G. Wells in the opening lines of his classic *The War of the Worlds*, 'that this world was being watched keenly and closely by intelligences greater than man's … Yet across the gulf of space … intellects vast and cool and unsympathetic, regarded this earth with envious eyes, and slowly and surely drew their plans against us.'

Wells was using science fiction to make a serious point. His saga plays out in a contemporary England invaded – and defeated – by the superior technology of an alien expeditionary force that arrived unheralded in a fleet of ships from a point of origin unimaginably distant. What ensues is a war of extermination; the interlopers are the vanguard of a colonial project intended to reshape our world in their image. Wells was trying to bring home to Victorian readers, the beneficiaries of imperialism, what life was like on the receiving end of that process.

The indigenous peoples of Mesoamerica needed no such literary metaphor. They had been living that reality for generations, ever since their mightiest nation, the Mexica of Tenochtitlan, had been humbled by the superior technology of an alien expeditionary force that arrived unheralded in a fleet of ships from a point of origin unimaginably distant. These were the Conquistadors, a handful of freebooting Spaniards whose ambition,

Tenochtitlan means 'place of the wild prickly pear cactus'. According to the origin myth of the Mexica, the city was founded through the bitter strife between their patron god, Huitzilopochtli, and his sister Malinalxochitl. Copil, the son of Malinalxochitl, conspired with the peoples of Azcapotzalco, Tlacopan, Coyoacán, Xochimilco, Culhuacan, and Chalco in a bid to destroy the Mexica, who took refuge in Tacuba. In revenge, they slew Copil. After removing his heart, Huitzilopochtli ordered a priest to stand in the reeds of Lake Texcoco and throw it with all his might. A prickly pear cactus would sprout from the heart, and in that place the Mexica would build their city. They would recognize the site because an eagle clutching a serpent would be perched on the prickly pear cactus. This tableau in modern Mexico City commemorates the moment the Mexica fulfilled this prophecy. (Author's collection)

5

Model of a *chinampa*. The southern two extensions of Lake Texcoco, Xochimilco and Chalco, were devoted to aquaculture (*chinampas*), irrigated gardens of relatively uniform size and laid out in a regular pattern, testament to centralized state planning. Adding the 9,500 hectares (over 2.3 million acres) of the *chinampas* in these two lakes to the agricultural potential of the Valley of Mexico went a long way towards supplying Tenochtitlan's needs. But still more food was required by the growing capital, and it could come only from the lands of the Mexica's tributaries. (Museo del Templo Mayor, Mexico City – author's collection)

Detail from the Stone of Tizoc, a *temalacatl* (raised circular fighting platform) on which sacrificial victims would fight to the death in gladiatorial combats. Surrounding the stone are 15 pairs of carved figures, each comprised of a Mexica warrior holding a captive by the hair, the symbol of defeat and submission in Mexica culture. Crowned with the hummingbird headdress of the god Huitzilopochtli, Tizoc, the seventh *huey tlatoani* or ruler (1481–86), is identified by his bleeding-leg name glyph. (Museo Nacional de Antropologia, Mexico City – author's collection)

opportunism, and good fortune brought down an empire and opened up a continent.

The Mexica enter history during the unsettled period following the collapse of Toltec hegemony over Mesoamerica during the 12th century. According to the most accepted chronology, the tribe migrated from their quasi-legendary homeland of Aztlan in the year 1 Flint (1168), led by four priests carrying the sacred bundle portraying Huitzilopochtli, their patron god. (Reference to their ancestral motherland led to the misnomer 'Aztec' – meaning 'inhabitant of Aztlan' – being applied to the Mexica of Tenochtitlan.) Their migration ended when Tenochtitlan ('the place of the wild prickly pear cactus') was founded in the year 2 House (1325).

The dominant power on the shores of Lake Texcoco during the 14th century were the Tepanecs of Azcapotzalco; two lords of this city, Acolnahuacatl (1304–63) and Tezozomoc (1363–1426), governed for more than a century. The Mexica served Azcapotzalco in a subordinate military role throughout this period, and their first three *tlatoani* (speakers) – Acamapichtli (1375–95), Huitzilihuitl (1396–1417) and Chimalpopoca (1417–27) – were tributaries to the Tepanecs.

Everything changed when Tezozomoc died and his sons fought to inherit his throne. In the ensuing conflict, Chimalpopoca was killed and Itzcoatl (1427–40) succeeded as the first independent Mexica *huey tlatoani* (great speaker). He forged a coalition between the cities of Tenochtitlan, Texcoco, and Tacuba that defeated and subjugated Azcapotzalco in 1428 and in succeeding years conquered Xochimilco and Coyoacán. This transformative event, which completely revolutionized the balance of power in Mesoamerica, would have an enduring legacy; long after

Tenochtitlan had fully subordinated its partners, the Mexica Empire would still be referred to as the Triple Alliance.

A new phase of expansion commenced ten years into the reign of the fifth *huey tlatoani*, Moctezuma I (1440–69). In order to reduce the vulnerability of the Mexica heartland to drought or other environmental factors, the Triple Alliance conquered the major grain-producing polities centered on Chalco, the Toluca Valley to the west, and Totonacapan ('the place of our sustenance') to the east, which brought the empire to the coast on the Gulf of Mexico.

The sixth *huey tlatoani*, Axayácatl (1469–81), was no less dedicated to this policy of expansion, forcibly reabsorbing Tlatelolco in 1473, but during his reign the Mexica suffered their first significant reversal on the battlefield, an invasion of Michoacán in 1479 that was routed by the rival Purépecha (Tarascan) Empire. The seventh *huey tlatoani*, Tizoc (1481–86), accomplished nothing, but his successor

The final battle of the legendary Tlaxcala warrior Tlahuicole, as depicted in the Government Palace, Tlaxcala. Captured by the Mexica in 1516, he accepted command of their expedition against the Purépecha (Tarascan) Empire over the dishonour of being ransomed back to his people. Hoping to meet a glorious demise in battle, he won several victories and returned to Tenochtitlan laden with spoils and a long train of captives. Refusing further honours at the hand of Moctezuma II, he insisted on the gladiatorial death fitting his rank. Tethered to the *temalacatl* in the temple complex, he defeated eight elite Mexica warriors in succession (note their bodies, stacked neatly at the base of the gladiatorial stone) before finally being overwhelmed. (Scala/Art Resource, NY)

as eighth *huey tlatoani*, Ahuitzotl (1486–1502), was a great conqueror who campaigned from one ocean to the other, warring with the Mixtec and Zapotec, imposing hegemony over Oaxaca, Tehuantepec, and even far-flung Soconusco, in the process absorbing great stretches of the Pacific coast into the imperial orbit.

When Moctezuma II (1502–20) succeeded as ninth *huey tlatoani* in the year 10 Rabbit, he inherited a war machine that could boast a proud heritage of almost unbroken success. He utilized this effectively to subdue vast swathes of territory to the south of Tenochtitlan. Mexica campaigns elsewhere, however, were less conclusive. Above all, the confederated tribes of the Tlaxcala stubbornly resisted all efforts to subdue them. In response, Moctezuma II initiated a succession of ceremonial flower wars against Tlaxcala, supplemented by an economic blockade that cut it off from trade in cotton and salt. Unable to land a killing blow or turn his enemies against each other through diplomacy, he would slowly squeeze them into submission.

There were troubles closer to home, even within the Triple Alliance itself. In 1516, on the death of Nezahualpilli, *tlatoani* of Texcoco, civil war erupted between his sons Coanacochtzin and Ixtlilxochitl. A compromise was eventually brokered that elevated another brother, Cacamatzin (Moctezuma II's nephew), to the throne but left Ixtlilxochitl in possession of the territories he had seized. Ixtlilxochitl therefore emerged from the conflict with both an independent powerbase and a grudge against the *huey tlatoani*.

Aside from his filial obligations, Moctezuma II's support of his nephew reflected his general philosophy towards governance, which emphasized

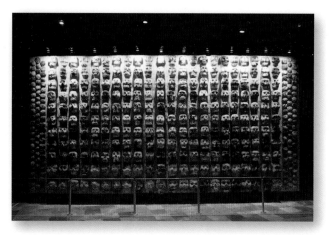

the centralization of power. He imposed a more sharply defined class stratification across Mexica society, marginalizing the *calpolli* (the quasi-autonomous communal ward administrations of Tenochtitlan) and excluding commoners from positions of authority in favour of the nobility. The intent was to accelerate the integration of the empire by attracting sons of the regional governing elites to Tenochtitlan, where they could be indoctrinated (in addition to being held hostage) and emerge loyal to the *huey tlatoani*.

A stone skull rack, or *tzompantli*. This was a symbolic representation of the Mexica obsession with death. Wars were not necessarily fought exclusively to take prisoners. During his conquest of the Pacific coastal towns to the south, for example, Ahuitzotl gave orders to kill everyone and take no captives, because the campaign was too far from home. But at more convenient locations, the army was instructed not to kill any of the captives on site but to bring them all back to Tenochtitlan. (Museo del Templo Mayor, Mexico City – author's collection)

Whatever the ultimate implications of its social evolution, the Mexica achievement in the first years of the 16th century was the greatest triumph of imperial endeavour in the history of Mesoamerica. Its armies spread terror from coast to coast, its bustling markets circulated goods from all over the known world, and its temples towered over the glittering jewel that was Tenochtitlan.

This triumph was under stress, however. There were famines in 1505, 1506, and 1514; earthquakes in 1507, 1512, and 1513; a harsh winter in 1511/12. And the people were uneasy, unable to shake off ill omens of some looming catastrophe. A comet illuminated the night sky. The temple of Huitzilopochtli burned atop its pyramid. A flood inundated much of the city. And then, in the spring of 1518, a peasant arrived at the imperial court from the Atlantic coast with a portent of doom; that there were mountains floating in the sea. Moctezuma II dispatched one of his four chief advisers, Teoctlamacazqui, Keeper of the House of Darkness (*tlillancalqui*), to confirm the tale. He returned with an ominous report: 'It is true that there have come to the shore I do not know what kind of people.'

Detail of the *tzompantli*, Museo del Templo Mayor, Mexico City. The heads of those who were sacrificed – called *xipemeh* and *tototectin* – were skinned, the flesh was dried, and the skulls were placed on the *tzompantli*. Cortés wrote that 'not one year has passed … in which three or four thousand souls have not been sacrificed in this manner.' (CatmenGata/Wikimedia Commons/CC-BY-SA-3.0)

The Mexica, at their imperial apogee, had made first contact with the rising power of Spain. Following up on the chance encounter with the New World by Christopher Columbus in 1492, the Spanish had colonized, exploited, and depopulated Hispaniola, advancing their flag throughout the Caribbean to Puerto Rico (1508), Jamaica (1509), and Cuba (1511). Always their sights were set on new frontiers, new lands to settle, new gold to acquire, new souls to save, new peoples to enslave. By 1513, Ponce de León had reconnoitred as far north as the coast of Florida, while Vasco Núñez de Balboa had crossed the isthmus as far south as Panama and become the first European to lay eyes on the Pacific Ocean.

Diego Velázquez de Cuéllar, the conqueror and lieutenant governor of Cuba, burned with the same desire to write himself into the pages of history. He authorized expeditions to explore the western reaches of the Caribbean by Francisco Hernández de Córdoba in 1517 and Juan de Grijalva the following year. These returned from the mainland reporting that it harboured great peril – when Córdoba provoked the indigenous Maya, his men were nearly wiped out and he himself expired from his wounds shortly after reporting back to Velázquez – but also the promise of unprecedented rewards in gold, cultivated lands, and the people to work them. Velázquez set in motion a third, and final, exploratory expedition that would lay the groundwork for his own subsequent grand campaign of conquest. The selection of Hernan Cortés to command this expedition was recommended by key deputies to Velázquez, not least because, according to Bernal Díaz, Cortés 'had promised to share equally with them all the profits arising from the gold, silver, and jewels' he anticipated acquiring on his expedition. Only through such dangling of the lure of exotic wealth was Cortés able to attract volunteers and outfit his expedition for, as Díaz continues, he 'was at that time greatly pinched for money to purchase the things he required, being, in addition, head and ears in debt'.

The extensive preparations undertaken by Cortés (for example, in commissioning native women to manufacture jackets of quilted cotton armour for the men under his command) were far in excess of those required to fulfil the limited mandate for the expedition as specified by Velázquez, who determined to relieve Cortés of command. He was moments too late, arriving at the dock on 18 November just as Cortés stepped into a boat heading for his flagship. 'How is this, compadre, that you are now setting off?' called Velázquez from the quay. Cortés merely shouted back that everything was going according to plan, and gave the order to hoist sail.

After stopping for additional food, men, and supplies at Pilón on Cape Cruz, further west at Trinidad, and then San Cristóbal de la Habana, the flotilla embarked for the Yucatan Peninsula, landing at Cozumel, then proceeding west along the coast, from La Isla de Mujeres to Cape Catoche to Campeche and

The base of the Templo Mayor, Mexico City. The serpent heads symbolize the sacred character of the structure as Coatepec, 'Serpent Hill', the setting for the birth of Huitzilopochtli and the mythic battle in which he defeated and dismembered his sister Coyolxauhqui. (Author's collection)

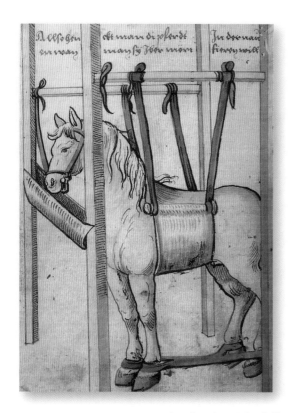

Cortés embarked for Mesoamerica with only 16 horses. Each would have been hoisted onboard by pulleys and confined for the duration of the voyage in the elaborate harness depicted in this contemporary illustration by Weiditz Trachtenbuch. They were expensive (costing at least 3,000 pesos apiece, more than the price for an African slave) and difficult to maintain. But their contribution to the Conquest would be invaluable. (Wikimedia Commons/ Public domain)

then on to Tabasco. Here, Cortés disembarked and moved inland to the trading centre at Potonchán, seizing it on 24 March after a sharp engagement with the indigenous Maya. The Spaniards were drawn into a major battle near the village of Centla on 28 March, securing victory the following day when Cortés unleashed his cavalry, the first time horses had been deployed for battle on the American mainland. Despite massively outnumbering the Conquistadors, the Maya were unable to kill any of them, while leaving hundreds of their own dead behind. Cortés accepted their submission at Potonchan. The tribute offered by the Maya included slave girls, one of whom, Malintzin, could speak Nahuatl, the language of the Mexica Empire to the west.

Cortés sailed on and, passing the mouth of the Tlacotalpan River, on Maundy Thursday, 20 April, he reached the island which Grijalva the year before had christened San Juan de Ulúa. This was offshore the town of Chalchicueyecan (the modern port of Veracruz) in Totonac territory, subject to Tenochtitlan. Here, Cortés met and exchanged gifts with emissaries from the local Mexica governor, Tendile, who resided some 20 miles away at Cuetlaxtlán. The following day, Good Friday, Cortés came ashore. Over the next two days, he entertained more Mexica, meeting with Tendile himself on Easter Sunday. Cortés made sure to intimidate his guests with a display of the firepower at his disposal. He stated outright his intention to proceed inland and meet with the Mexica head of state. And he made no secret of his motivation: 'I and my companions suffer from a disease of the heart which can be cured only with gold.'

Tendile reported this exchange, and everything else he had witnessed – the horses, the guns – to Moctezuma II in Tenochtitlan. The *huey tlatoani* was paralyzed with indecision. What, exactly, was he dealing with? Having been trained in the priesthood, he could not discount the possibility that the strangers were not men but gods. In the Mexica calendar, 1519 was equivalent to the year 1 Reed, which was associated with the god Quetzalcoatl. This was ominous because, according to the *Codex Chimalpopoca*:

> If he comes on 1 Crocodile, he strikes the old men, the old women;
> If on 1 Jaguar, 1 Deer, 1 Flower, he strikes at children;
> If on 1 Reed, he strikes at kings.

Moctezuma II settled on a policy of appeasement. He dispatched Teoctlamacazqui at the head of a retinue of over 100 bearers, laden with gorgeous and extravagant gifts for Cortés. If the newcomer was a divine being, he would be satisfied with such tribute; if a man, overawed by the majesty on display. Either way, he must depart; Moctezuma II would not receive him.

This offering had the opposite to its intended effect. Far from having cowed Cortés, the quality – and quantity – of the treasure on display had only convinced him the wealth of the empire was his for the taking. But before he could penetrate into the interior, he needed to secure his position on the coast, both physically and politically. The Conquistadors founded a town, christened Villa Rica de la Vera Cruz, and voted in a suite of officers, who in turn elected Cortés their captain-general. This gave him legal cover to escape his commission from Velázquez and go over the heads of the colonial administrators in the Caribbean by claiming to act directly in the name of King Charles V. He also began cultivating allies. The local Totonac people were unwilling subjects of the Mexica. Cortés incited them to rise up against their overseers, knowing this would invite retaliation, thus leaving the Totonacs no choice but to seek support from the Spaniards.

The Calendar Stone at the Museo Nacional de Antropologia, Mexico City. In the centre of the monolith is the face of the solar deity, Tonatiuh, holding a human heart in each of his clawed hands; his tongue is represented by a stone sacrificial knife (*tecpatl*). The four squares that surround Tonatiuh represent the four previous eras, each of which ended with the destruction of the world and humanity. The object may have served as a *temalacatl*. (Museo del Templo Mayor, Mexico City – author's collection)

Cortés ordered the Totonac tribes to convene in the city of Cempoala, where they accepted Spanish secular and religious authority. The time had come to march on Tenochtitlan. Cortés (reinforced by a caravel from Cuba under the command of Francisco de Saucedo that arrived with 60 men and several horses) left behind 150 men under the command of Juan de Escalante to hold Villa Rica, compensating for their absence by drafting several hundred Totonacs to serve as bearers. His force, which was divided into companies of about 50 men each, captained by Pedro de Alvarado, Velázquez de León, Cristóbal de Olid, Alonso de Ávila, and Gonzalo de Sandoval, departed Cempoala on 16 August. To emphasize the all or nothing nature of his gamble, Cortés ordered the fleet scuttled. The Conquistadors would conquer or die in the attempt.

The trail west led up into the high Cordilleras. Conditions were harsh, but there was no resistance from any of the towns the column encountered en route. That changed when Cortés crossed into Tlaxcala territory.

Tlaxcala was a confederacy of four provinces – Quiyahuiztlan, Tepeticpac, Tizatlan, and Ocotelolco – each with its own lord (*tlatoque*). When the Spaniards arrived, Tizatlan's ruler, Xicotencatl the Elder, and Ocotelolco's ruler, Maxixcatl, were vying for dominance of the confederation. Maxixcatl's power was economic, because Ocotelolco was the site of the main market, whereas Xicotencatl the Elder's power lay with the military. Tizatlan controlled the army, whose leading commander was the king's 35-year-old son and heir apparent, Xicotencatl the Younger. Xicotencatl's decision to attack the Spaniards was guaranteed to put Maxixcatl in the opposition camp.

Cortés knew none of this, only that thousands of warriors – clearly veterans, ranked in disciplined formations – had appeared out of nowhere. They first lured his cavalry into an ambush, killing two horses, then launched a general assault that nearly overwhelmed the intruders. The Spaniards fought their way through to a deserted hilltop village, Tzompachtepetl, where they held on grimly as days stretched into weeks, dressing their wounds with body fat scavenged from the carcasses of slain foes, and burying their own dead

Though most modern Mexicans consider the Tlaxcala traitors for their role in the Conquest, their descendants don't see it that way at all. A series of frescoes painted by Desiderio Hernández Xochitiotzin for the Government Palace in Tlaxcala present their side of the story. This one, entitled 'The meeting of the Spanish and the Tlaxcala', depicts the Conquistadors working with a proud, sophisticated people who have embraced Spanish culture (note the prominence of the cross) while retaining their own distinct identity. Note also the theme of partnership, not subordination; Cortés is depicted (bottom right) respectfully accepting the terms of the alliance, not barking out orders to a subordinate race. (DeA Picture Library/Art Resource, NY)

secretly beneath a house to keep the Tlaxcala unaware of the extent to which their numbers were dwindling. At this point, Díaz readily concedes, 'the idea of penetrating into Mexico appeared to us perfectly laughable'. The survival of the expedition, let alone victory, would have been impossible without the support of the Totonacs; 'Had it not been for them,' one of Cortés' intimates, Francisco de Solis, baldly testified later about these battles, 'we should not have won'.

The Conquistadors were isolated and exposed, but try as they might, the Tlaxcala could not overcome them. The failure of an attempted incursion at night proved decisive. Xicotencatl the Younger was ordered to cease hostilities. When he ignored this directive, Chichimecateuctli, the commander of Ocotelolco's contingent, withdrew his forces, leaving Xicotencatl the Younger with too few men to guarantee victory, and no choice but to break off his attacks.

The fiercely independent Tlaxcala were bloodied, but unbowed. They could have continued the conflict indefinitely, but, having had a taste of Toledo steel, appreciated the potential of these interlopers as allies. Cortés now met with Xicotencatl the Elder and Maxixcatl as an invited guest, not a conqueror. While his men and beasts recovered, Cortés settled on terms with his hosts, who offered 6,000 warriors, plus guides and bearers for the advance on Tenochtitlan.

Cortés set out on 10 October, making for Cholula, the largest city in Mesoamerica outside of the Triple Alliance, a wealthy focus for trade, and a major pan-regional ceremonial centre, closely associated with the god Quetzalcoatl. Overlooking the entire city, Cholula's Great Pyramid was higher than its equivalent in Tenochtitlan (120 steps to 114) with a larger base than that of the Great Pyramid at Giza, making it the largest free-standing man-made edifice in the world.

After agreeing to post the Tlaxcala outside the city, the Conquistadors were comfortably housed and provisioned within. But then the supply of food dwindled until it stopped altogether. Cortés began receiving ominous reports from his Totonac and Tlaxcala allies that Cholula was conniving with the Mexica. Residents, carrying goods and possessions on their backs, were leaving Cholula; a number of the city's streets had been cordoned off, while those left open had been studded with pit traps lined with sharp stakes; stones were being piled on rooftops.

Cortés decided on swift and salutary action. He insisted the lords of Cholula meet him in the courtyard of the temple of Quetzalcoatl so he could formally take his leave of them before pressing on to Tenochtitlan. Over a hundred of them came, unarmed. The doors of the courtyard were then closed by the Spaniards. Cortés demanded to know why his hosts were conspiring against his life. They admitted their complicity, but insisted they were only acting on

Mesoamerica before the Spanish Conquest, 1519

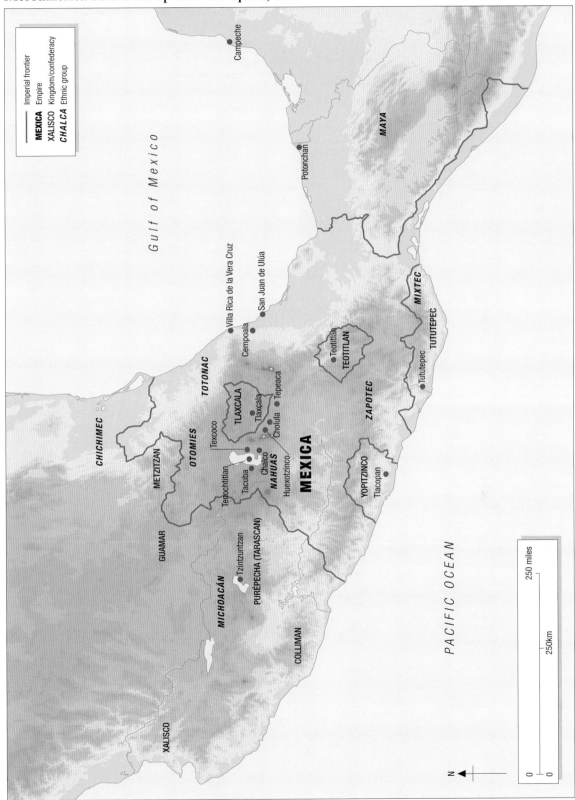

Legend:
- Imperial frontier
- Empire
- **MEXICA** Empire
- XALISCO Kingdom/confederacy
- *CHALCA* Ethnic group

Gulf of Mexico

PACIFIC OCEAN

Campeche

MAYA

Potonchan

Villa Rica de la Vera Cruz

San Juan de Ulúa

Cempoala

MIXTEC

TUTUTEPEC

Tututepec

Teotitlan

TEOTITLAN

TOTONAC

ZAPOTEC

TLAXCALA

Tlaxcala

Tepeaca

Cholula

Texcoco

CHICHIMEC

OTOMIES

METZTITZAN

Tenochtitlan

Tacuba

Chalco

MEXICA

NAHUAS

Huexotzinco

YOPITZINCO

Tlacopan

GUAMAR

Tzintzuntzan

MICHOACÁN

PURÉPECHA (TARASCAN)

COLLIMAN

XALISCO

N

250 miles

250km

250 miles

250km

a plot instigated by Moctezuma II. Cortés had heard enough. Starting with the assembled lords, the population was put to the sword. Cortés himself later admitted 3,000 were killed. His Tlaxcala and Totonac allies then sacked the city, torching the most important houses and temples.

Far from seizing on this desecration of a great city within the orbit of the Triple Alliance as a rallying cry, Moctezuma II responded by doubling down on his policy of appeasement. He dispatched gifts and apologised profusely to Cortés for the alleged conspiracy, which he ascribed to the leaders of the local Mexica garrisons at Izúcar and at Acatzinco.

Was this slaughter a justifiable pre-emptive response to a legitimate threat? Or was it premeditated grand strategy? Cholula had been a Tlaxcala ally until recently, when it defected to the Mexica, marking a significant shift in the strategic balance. Maxixcatl was tied by kinship to Cholula's previous ruling lineage. Restoring that dynasty to power would enable Tlaxcala to break the tightening Mexica siege, and greatly enhance Maxixcatl's prestige vis-à-vis Xicotencatl the Elder within the Tlaxcala confederacy. Cortés, too, stood to gain from the reduction of Cholula; he would not want to leave a Mexica ally straddling his supply and communications lines back to Villa Rica on the coast and otherwise threatening his rear once he marched on to Tenochtitlan.

Two things were certain. First, as Joan de Cáceres put it, the massacre was a *castigo* (punishment) that would have a significant deterrent effect on any communities contemplating resistance to the Spaniards in future. Alonso de la Serna confirmed the action in fact 'caused such fear that no one dared to commit such treason again'. Second, there could no longer be any confusion over whether Cortés was the reincarnation of, or envoy from, Quetzalcoatl, who could hardly have allowed the courtyard of his own temple to be so profaned.

Whoever Cortés was, he departed Cholula on 1 November, making for Tenochtitlan. Every gambit Moctezuma II had employed to turn the interlopers away – bribery, threats, sorcery, even the dispatch of an impersonator to carry out negotiations in his stead – had failed. He now convened his inner council to solicit its advice on what to do about the approaching aliens. His brother Cuitláhuac urged him to take action: 'I pray to our gods that you will not let the strangers into your house. They will cast you out of it and overthrow your rule, and when you try to recover what you have lost, it will be too late.' But his nephew Cacamatzin recommended a conciliatory approach, warning the *huey tlatoani* of the damage to his reputation if he were to repudiate the embassy of a distant power; the Mexica tributary states might interpret such an action as weakness, even cowardice. Moctezuma II accepted this perspective and gave orders Cortés was to be welcomed to Tenochtitlan.

Cortés was making informed judgements of his own. The main route from Cholula to Tenochtitlan was via a 3,000m-high pass to the north. The other road was narrower and offered a more difficult trek between Popocatépetl (the Hill that Smokes) and its

Detail of Mexica uniforms and shields, from the *Codex Mendoza* (Folio 20r), held in the Bodleian Library, Oxford. (Wikimedia Commons/ Public domain)

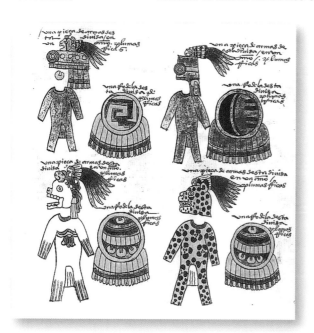

sister volcano Iztaccíhuatl (White Woman) through a 3,500m-high pass to the south. Choosing the latter route (ever since known as the Path of Cortés) cost the Spaniards their Totonac allies, who begged permission to return home. But the political advantages outweighed the physical challenges. Courtesy of his Tlaxcala allies, Cortés was aware that while the northern pass emptied out into the Texcoco area, which strongly supported the Triple Alliance, the southern alternative led to the Chalca city-states, which had been conquered by the Mexica in 1464 and resented their subordination.

Detail of Mexica uniforms and shields, from the *Codex Mendoza*. (Wikimedia Commons/Public domain)

The Spaniards hiked up into the mountains, entering *terra nullius*. After scouting ahead from the heights, Diego de Ordaz reported 'he had been staggered by what he had seen'. Alonso de Aguilar recalled, 'another new world of great cities and towers and a sea, and in the middle of it a very great city had been built and in truth it appeared to have caused him fear and astonishment'.

Descending into the Valley of Mexico, the Conquistadors spent two nights at Amecameca, then succeeding evenings at Chalco and Ayotzingo. Everywhere they went, 'we were astounded,' Bernal Díaz would reminisce. 'These great towns and temples had buildings rising from the water, all made of stone, and it seemed like an enchanted vision from the tale of Amadis. Indeed, some of our soldiers asked if this was not all a dream.' There was tension beneath the glitter, however. As Cortés had hoped, the local nobility complained bitterly about their oppression at the hands of the Mexica. Cortés assured them they would soon be free.

Detail of Mexica uniforms and shields, from the *Codex Mendoza*. (Wikimedia Commons/Public domain)

A Mexica delegation headed by Cacamatzin arrived and escorted the newcomers to Iztlapalapa, city of Cuitláhuac. The next day, 8 November, Cortés started along the causeway to Tenochtitlan, heading west to join the main north–south causeway from Coyoacán to the capital.

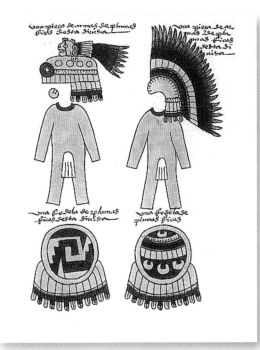

About a mile and a half short of the main gate, the expedition reached a place known as Acachinanco, the point where the causeway ended and the houses of the city began, guarded by a fort with two towers. This was the traditional place for greeting returning heroes. More ominously, it was also known as Malcuitlapilco, 'the tail end of the file of prisoners,' in reference to those destined for sacrifice at the inauguration of the Great Temple in 1487. An assembly of richly dressed Mexica nobles greeted the Conquistadors and led them over a drawbridge into the heart of the city. Here, at last, Cortés would come face to face with the figure he had sought since hearing the first awed whispers of his name: Moctezuma II, the *huey tlatoani* himself, was coming to meet him.

CHRONOLOGY

1000–1200	The Mexica depart their mythical homeland of Aztlan.
1200	The Mexica arrive in the Basin of Mexico and settle on the shores of Lake Texcoco.
1325	Tenochtitlan is founded.
1337	Tlatelolco declares independence from Tenochtitlan.
1375–95	Reign of Acamapichtli, first *huey tlatoani*.
1396–1417	Reign of Huitzilihuitl, second *huey tlatoani*.
1417–27	Reign of Chimalpopoca, third *huey tlatoani*.
1427–40	Reign of Itzcoatl, fourth *huey tlatoani*.
1428	Tenochtitlan, Texcoco, and Tacuba form the Triple Alliance and conquer Azcapotzalco.
1429	The Triple Alliance conquer Xochimilco.
1430	The Triple Alliance conquer Coyoacán.
1440–69	Reign of Moctezuma I, fifth *huey tlatoani*.
1467	Birth of Moctezuma II.
1469–81	Reign of Axayácatl, sixth *huey tlatoani*.
1473	Tlatelolco is forcibly reabsorbed by Tenochtitlan.
1479	The marriage of Ferdinand of Aragon and Isabella of Castile unifies their states in the Kingdom of Spain.
1481–86	Reign of Tizoc, seventh *huey tlatoani*.

1485	Birth of Hernan Cortés.
1486–1502	Reign of Ahuitzotl, eighth *huey tlatoani*.
1487	Ahuitzotl completes the Templo Mayor.
1488	Bartolomeu Dias rounds the Cape of Good Hope linking the Atlantic with Indian Ocean.
1492	Spain conquers Granada, completing the Reconquista.
1492–93	First voyage of Columbus.
1493–96	Second voyage of Columbus.
1494	Treaty of Tordesillas, an agreement between Spain and Portugal over ownership of newly discovered lands.
1497–99	Vasco da Gama rounds the Cape of Good Hope and forges the trade route connecting Europe with the Orient.
1498–1500	Third voyage of Columbus.
1502	Moctezuma II is elected ninth *huey tlatoani*.
1502–04	Fourth voyage of Columbus.
1507	Martin Waldseemüller publishes his *Universalis Cosmographia*; it is the first map of the world to include the name America, after the explorer Amerigo Vespucci.
1508	Ponce de León conquers Puerto Rico; Vicente Yáñez Pinzón and Juan Díaz de Solís reconnoitre the coast of Central America.
1509	Juan de Esquival conquers Jamaica.
1511	Diego Velázquez de Cuéllar conquers Cuba.

1513	Ponce de León reconnoitres the coast of Florida; Vasco Núñez de Balboa becomes the first European to encounter the Pacific Ocean.	28 March	First battle at Centla.
		29 March	Second battle at Centla.
		17 April	Palm Sunday: Cortés departs from Tabasco.
1515	Death of Nezahualpilli, *tlatoani* of Texcoco; civil war between his sons Cacamatzin and Ixtlilxochitl.	20 April	Maundy Thursday: Cortés arrives off San Juan de Ulúa; the expedition founds Villa Rica de la Vera Cruz.
1516	Charles I is proclaimed King of Spain.		
		21 April	On Good Friday, Cortés comes ashore at San Juan de Ulúa.
1517			
8 February	Francisco Hernández de Córdoba sails from Cuba; he arrives off the Yucatan Peninsula at the end of the month.	3 June	Cortés reaches Cempoala.
		28 June	Charles I of Spain is elected Charles V, Holy Roman Emperor; Villa Rica de la Vera Cruz is formally founded.
29 March	Córdoba reaches Campeche.		
20 April	Córdoba returns to Cuba.	10 July	Members of the expedition petition the Spanish Crown for recognition as a separate colony.
1518			
3 May	Juan de Grijalva arrives off Cozumel.	16 August	Cortés departs Cempoala for the Mexican interior.
31 May	Grijalva reaches Laguna de Términos.		
11 June	Grijalva reaches Coatzacoalco.	2 September	Cortés fights his first battle with the Tlaxcala.
23 October	Diego Velázquez, lieutenant governor of Cuba, commissions Hernan Cortés to lead a third expedition to the mainland.	23 September	Cortés enters Tlaxcala.
		10 October	Cortés departs Tlaxcala for Cholula.
15 November	Grijalva returns to Cuba.	12 October	Cortés enters Cholula.
18 November	Cortés sails from Santiago de Cuba. His expedition completes fitting out at Trinidad and San Cristóbal de la Habana.	18 October	Massacre at Cholula.
		1 November	Cortés departs Cholula.
1519		8 November	Cortés enters Tenochtitlan and encounters Moctezuma II.
10 February	Cortés sails for Mexico.	14 November	Cortés seizes Moctezuma II.
14 March	Cortés departs from Cozumel.	**1520**	
22 March	Cortés lands in Tabasco.	5 March	Pánfilo de Narváez departs Cuba on a mission to intercept Cortés.
24 March	On Annunciation Day, Cortés takes the town of Potonchan; Doña Marina joins the expedition.	19 April	Narváez arrives at San Juan de Ulúa.

16 May	Festival of Toxcatl: Pedro de Alvarado massacres the Mexica nobility.
28–29 May	Cortés defeats Narváez at Cempoala.
24 June	Cortés returns to Tenochtitlan.
25 June	Cortés releases Cuitláhuac, who assumes power as acting *huey tlatoani* in Tenochtitlan. The Mexica rise up against Cortés and commence laying siege to the Palace of Axayácatl.
27 June	Moctezuma II is wounded.
28 June	Failed attempt to break out of Tenochtitlan by the Spaniards.
29 June	Battle at the Temple of Yopico.
30 June	Death of Moctezuma II.
1 July	*La Noche Triste* (the Night of Sorrow): the Spaniards break out of Tenochtitlan, but at a terrible cost.
7 July	The Spaniards defeat the Mexica at Otumba near Lake Texcoco.
11 July	The Spaniards arrive at Tlaxcala.
1 August	Cortés marches against Tepeaca.
7 August	Cortés conquers Tepeaca.
4 September	Cortés founds Segura de la Frontera on the site of Tepeaca.
August–September	Cortés campaigns in the region surrounding Tepeaca.
16 September	Cuitláhuac formally succeeds as tenth *huey tlatoani*.
September–November	Smallpox devastates Tenochtitlan.
December	Cortés dispatches Gonzalo de Sandoval to secure Zautla and Xalacingo.
4 December	Death of Cuitláhuac; Cuauhtémoc

	is elected his successor and formally succeeds as the eleventh *huey tlatoani* in February.
13 December	Cortés departs Tepeaca for Tlaxcala.
28 December	Cortés commences his campaign against Tenochtitlan.
31 December	Cortés takes and sacks Texcoco.

1521

Early January	Cortés takes and sacks Iztlapalapa.
Late January	Sandoval drives the Mexica out of Chalco.
Early February	Cortés takes and sacks Tacuba.
18 February	Cortés returns to Texcoco.
25 March	Sandoval defeats the Mexica at Chalco.
5 April	Cortés departs Texcoco for Chalco.
13 April	Cortés takes and sacks Cuernavaca.
16 April	Cortés takes and sacks Xochimilco.
18 April	Cortés occupies Coyoacán.
22 April	Cortés returns to Texcoco.
28 April	Spanish brigantines launched on Lake Texcoco.
22 May	Cortés dispatches columns under Alvarado and Cristóbal de Olid against Tenochtitlan.
25 May	Alvarado and Olid occupy Tacuba.
26 May	Alvarado and Olid destroy the aqueduct at Chapultepec, severing the supply of fresh water into Tenochtitlan.
31 May	A column under Sandoval occupies Iztlapalapa.
1 June	Cortés initiates the naval campaign

	on Lake Texcoco while his lieutenants secure the causeways; the siege of Tenochtitlan commences.	1527–28	Narváez fails to establish a colony in Florida.
10 June	A major Allied incursion into Tenochtitlan reaches the temple complex before withdrawing.	1528	Cortés returns to Spain, where Charles V appoints him Marquis of the Valley of Oaxaca; Sandoval dies of illness.
15 June	The second major Allied incursion again reaches the temple complex, and again withdraws.	1529–31	Nuño de Guzmán campaigns in western Mexico.
		1530	Cortés returns to Mexico.
23 June	The Mexica repulse the Allied incursion under Alvarado.	1532	Francisco Pizarro campaigns against the Inca Empire.
30 June	The Mexica repulse the Allied incursion under Cortés, inflicting significant losses.	1533	Fortún Ximénez encounters the Baja California Peninsula.
21 July	Allied spearheads clear the entire road to Tacuba, linking their columns; the Palace of Cuauhtémoc is burned.	1535	Cortés reconnoitres the Baja California Peninsula.
		1539	Francisco de Ulloa maps the Baja Peninsula.
25 July	The Mexica lose control of the great market in Tlatelolco; seven-eighths of Tenochtitlan is now under Allied occupation.	1539–42	Hernando de Soto campaigns in the south-eastern United States.
		1540–42	Francisco Vázquez de Coronado campaigns in the south-western United States.
12 August	Negotiations fail; the Allied offensive shatters the last Mexica defensive line.		
13 August	Cuauhtémoc, the last *huey tlatoani*, surrenders Tenochtitlan to Cortés; end of the Mexica Empire.	1541	Cortés returns to Spain; Alvarado succumbs to combat wounds in Mexico; Pizarro is assassinated in Peru.
1522	Alvarado campaigns against the Mixtec and Zapotec city-states in Oaxaca; Olid campaigns in Jalisco and Colima in western Mexico.	1541–42	Francisco de Orellana navigates the length of the Amazon River.
		1542	Juan Rodriguez Cabrillo reconnoitres the coast of California.
1523	Olid campaigns in Honduras; he declares independence from Spanish authority.	1547	Death of Cortés on 2 December.
1524–26	Cortés campaigns in Honduras.	1560–61	Lope de Aguirre navigates the length of the Orinoco River, murders his superiors, exterminates indigenous tribes, rebels against the Spanish crown, seizes Isla Margarita, attacks Panama, and kills his own daughter rather than surrender her, before finally being captured and executed; end of the Conquistador era.
1525	Olid is defeated, captured, and executed.		
1526	Lucas Vázquez de Ayllón fails to establish a colony in the Carolinas.		

Spanish exploration and settlement to 1519

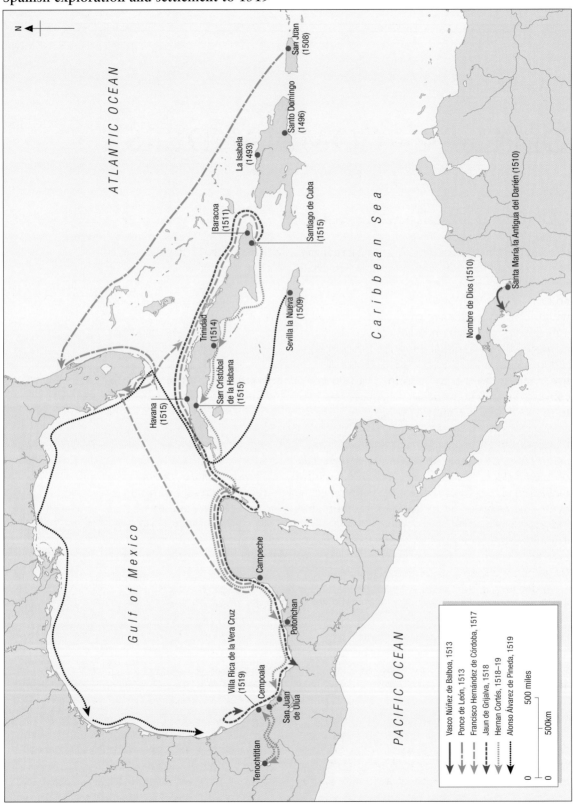

OPPOSING COMMANDERS

CONQUISTADORS AND ALLIES

Hernan Cortés de Monroy y Pizarro Altamirano stands incontestably as one of the great military captains in history. His credentials as a warlord when he departed Cuba for the Mesoamerican mainland were non-existent. He had no formal authority; he was an ambassador without a commission, a general without a rank, with no intelligence concerning his theatre of operations, and only a handful of men under his command. Yet, by sheer force of personality he forged a multinational coalition that brought down an empire and would reshape a continent. As Francisco López de Gómara wrote in 1552, 'Long live, then, the name and memory of him who conquered so vast a land, converted such a multitude of men, cast down so many idols, and put an end to so much sacrifice and the eating of human flesh!'

Born in 1485 in Medellín, Extremadura, he was the only son of a *hidalgo*, a minor noble. After some schooling in the law, Cortés emigrated in 1506 to Santo Domingo, where he was appointed *escribano* (notary) in the new town of Azúa de Compostela. Five years later, he enlisted with Diego Velázquez de Cuéllar in his conquest of Cuba. The acting lieutenant governor subsequently made Cortés his secretary and granted him an *encomienda* (estate, and the indigenous population to work it). However, the two men would cultivate a rocky relationship, with Velázquez at one point ordering his subordinate arrested on charges of conspiring against him, then promoting him to *alcalde* (chief magistrate) of Santiago de Cuba.

A devout Catholic and inveterate bigamist, a crusader and an opportunist, a renegade and an imperialist, Cortés was a man of many contradictions. 'I look on it as better to be rich in fame than in goods,' he once wrote to his father, yet his lust for gold was at least equal to his desire for glory. He had little military experience, but Velázquez knew that Cortés had profited from his mining and ranching enterprises to such an extent that he could personally afford to invest heavily in an expedition to mainland Mesoamerica.

It was there the real Cortés emerged, with the unheralded genius for improvisation and initiative that defines the movers and shakers of history. By word or deed – rousing, cajoling, bribing, threatening, punishing – he had the innate, instinctive capacity to outmanoeuvre his enemies and inspire his friends at the crucial moment. Alonso de Aguilar recalled Cortés addressing his rank and file on the eve of a battle – typically, against great odds – by 'leading us to believe that each one of us would be a count or duke and one

This anonymous portrait of Hernan Cortés reflects the physical attributes his contemporaries recorded of him. When the Conquistadors departed Cuba for the unknown, he was 'fairly thin' and 'of medium stature, somewhat bent, without much of a beard'. He is depicted here in formal dress, suitable for the court of King Charles V, and without any evidence of the scars he earned on campaign in Mexico. These included his fingers being crushed defending the Palace of Axayácatl; his skull being fractured during the retreat after *La Noche Triste*; and his leg being wounded when he was nearly taken at the breach in the causeway to Tlatelolco. (Album/Art Resource, NY)

of the titled; with this he transformed us from lambs to lions, and we went out against that large army without fear or hesitation'.

Cortés was not infallible, and sometimes his natural predilection for unstinting aggression in the field could prove costly, as Díaz found out when he participated in the frontal assault up the precipitous slopes at Tlaycapan, where the defenders could roll boulders down at the Spaniards clambering hand over hand up towards them: 'It is a miracle we were not all crushed to pieces; and certainly Cortés had, in this instance, not acted as a prudent general when he ordered this perilous attack.' He also allowed himself to be persuaded into accelerating the reduction of Tenochtitlan with a precipitate assault on the ceremonial core of Tlatelolco, which culminated in the costliest setback of the siege, and on more than one occasion his impetuous leadership from the front nearly cost him his life. Overall, however – his reputation for spontaneous belligerence notwithstanding – it was his capacity to define and apply a grand strategic vision that enabled his ultimate triumph over the Mexica. Throughout the bitter weeks of street fighting for Tenochtitlan, Díaz recalled Cortés 'was always writing to us to tell us all what we were to do and how we were to fight'. His talent for diplomacy, and skill in extracting maximum value from indigenous allies; his understanding the fundamentals of logistics and supply chains; and his boldness in adding a naval dimension to the campaign, all ensured victory would be inevitable and entirely on his terms.

Of course, no man ever won a campaign on his own. Cortés was the driving force of the Conquest, but 'it must also be remembered,' in the words of Díaz, 'that he had the good fortune to command officers and soldiers on whom he could place every reliance under all circumstances, who not only lent a powerful arm in battle, but likewise assisted him with their prudent counsel'.

The most prominent of the Conquistadors, **Pedro de Alvarado**, was dubbed *Tonatiuh*, sun god, by the Mexica in homage to his red-blond hair. Cortés made much use of him throughout the campaign (though was oddly reticent to give him much credit; it was not until 1528, in his fourth dispatch to King Charles V, that Cortés reported Alvarado's exploits), but their partnership worked best when Cortés kept his subordinate on a very tight leash.

Alvarado's first experience of Mesoamerica came in 1518 when he captained one of the vessels under Juan de Grijalva. Alvarado's early return from that expedition, and bad-mouthing of his erstwhile commander, played a significant role in alienating Velázquez from Grijalva and the subsequent appointment of Cortés to lead the expedition in 1519. They were peers (both aged 34 in the first year of the Conquest) and, always, Alvarado was the most loyal of his officers to Cortés. That and his prowess in battle led to his being deputized with significant responsibilities. But leaving Alvarado behind to manage Tenochtitlan when Cortés marched against Pánfilo de Narváez (whom Velázquez had dispatched to arrest Cortés) was a critical error; administration and diplomacy were not his strong suits. Upon his return, Cortés demanded an explanation for the Toxcatl massacre. According to Díaz, Alvarado attempted to justify his actions as representing pre-emptive self-defence, a response that was 'by no means satisfactory to Cortés,' who responded, 'rather sharply, that he saw very little truth in all this, but a good deal of irregularity hurtful to the Spanish cause'. But for all his faults, Cortés needed Alvarado. He did not dismiss him from command then, nor later, when, during the siege of Tenochtitlan, Alvarado pushed too deep into the city and suffered a serious reverse. For Cortés, it was always better to err on the side of being too aggressive than too passive.

Bernal Díaz described Pedro de Alvarado as 'in every sense beautifully proportioned in body, noble in his gait,' with 'very pleasing features, and an amiable manner of expressing himself, so that there always appeared a smile on his countenance'. He was also fearless, impetuous, cruel, and utterly amoral. After the defeat of the Mexica, Alvarado went on to subdue Tehuantepec and the Mixtec region of Oaxaca. After several other campaigns, by order of Cortés he left Mexico City in December of 1523 to undertake the conquest of Guatemala, the title to which he was granted in 1527 when he sailed for Spain and was appointed Governor of the region. Alvarado was still campaigning at the age of 56 when he was crushed under his mortally wounded horse, dying several days later in Guadalajara. (De Agostini Picture Library/ Bridgeman Images)

Gonzalo de Sandoval was still very young when the expedition set out, but he rose in rank – and responsibility – over the course of the campaign, 'when we saw all his real qualities developed in a manner that drew forth unbounded praise from Cortés and every soldier,' Díaz noted. His coolness and competence culminated in his being recognized as the effective deputy to Cortés, despite the fact of his always giving the impression he had 'reneged on divine Providence,' and was incessantly 'speaking ill of Our Lord God and his blessed Mother'.

Another young Conquistador, **Andrés de Tapia**, was only 24 when he signed up with Cortés, emerging as one of his most trusted captains over the course of the campaign. **Alonso de Aguilar** also distinguished himself for his integrity and quiet valour, and was given such responsible assignments as guarding Moctezuma II when Cortés ordered his imprisonment. **Cristóbal de Olid**, 'a man of great courage and energy,' as Díaz called him, sailed with Cortés as his quartermaster, though his outstanding service against the Mexica was later overshadowed by his treason. Lastly, through his herculean efforts to construct the fleet of brigantines that enabled the Conquistadors to dominate Lake Texcoco, **Martín López** perhaps contributed more to the subjugation of Tenochtitlan than anyone else under Cortés.

However, of all his subordinates, Spanish men or those native to the New World, none was more important to Cortés than a singular indigenous woman, who went by many titles. Her original name was **Malinali**, and

Morion helmet, on display in the Palace of the Grand Master, Valletta, Malta. These would come to define Spanish armies later in the 16th century, but the men accompanying Cortés would have worn much simpler styles. Most Conquistadors transitioned to indigenous cotton armour over the course of the Conquest, but all would have retained steel protection for their heads, if nothing else. (Author's collection)

she was of royal stock. Her father had been *tlatoani* of Painala while her mother ruled in Xaltipan. After her father died, her mother remarried another local lord, to whom she bore a son. In order to smooth this boy's succession to all three titles, Malinali's mother publicly gave out her daughter was dead while privately selling her into the slave trade. When the Conquistadors arrived, she was living among the Chontal Mayas of Potonchan, who gifted her to Cortés. He initially paired her off with Alonso Hernández Puertocarrero, only to reclaim her when Puertocarrero was dispatched as an emissary to the court in Madrid. From that point, she was 'always in my company,' as Cortés noted to King Charles V. Christened **Doña Marina** after her baptism, the Mexica recognized her regal status with the honorific suffix *-tzin*, hence **Malintzin**, which the Spanish interpreted as **Malinche**.

Whatever her title, Díaz wrote that she possessed 'manly valour,' and 'betrayed no weakness but a courage greater than that of a woman'. This made her 'a valuable instrument to us in the conquest of New Spain. It was, through her only, under the protection of the Almighty, that many things were accomplished by us: without her we never should have understood the Mexican language, and, upon the whole, have been unable to surmount many difficulties.'

The triumph of Cortés would have been impossible without the support of the Tlaxcala, whose field commander during the siege of Tenochtitlan was **Chichimecatecle**. But it was Cortés' most dedicated indigenous ally **Ixtlilxochitl** who, as one biographer concluded, emerged from the saga of the Conquest with 'the melancholy glory of contributing more than any chieftain of America to enslave his countrymen'. Though still only a teenager, in 1516 he contested with his brother Coanacochtzin for the succession to his father Nezahualpilli as *tlatoani* of Texcoco, only for Moctezuma II to impose a compromise choice, another brother, Cacamatzin. After repudiating this settlement, Ixtlilxochitl emerged from the ensuing civil war with some territorial authority in an uneasy power-sharing arrangement. When Cacamatzin was murdered by the Spaniards during the Toxcatl massacre, Coanacochtzin assumed power in Texcoco, only to flee with the Mexica loyalists to Tenochtitlan when Cortés marched on the Valley of Mexico, effectively ceding authority to Ixtlilxochitl. Coanacochtzin remained formally in office after the Mexica were defeated until he and his fellow puppet monarchs Tetlepanquetzatzin of Tacuba and Cuauhtémoc of Tenochtitlan were forced to accompany Cortés on his 1525 expedition against Honduras. There, far from their homes, Cortés had them executed on manufactured charges of conspiracy. Cortés subsequently confirmed Ixtlilxochitl as *tlatoani* of Texcoco, where he reigned until his death in 1531.

With all the fervour of the newly converted, Ixtlilxochitl, who had accepted baptism, adopted Conquistador methods in addition to their cause. Having taken a Mexica officer captive during the siege of Tenochtitlan, the chronicles relate 'he had a great many dry reeds brought and thrown over the captain, and burned him alive,' telling any witnesses to inform Cuauhtémoc 'and his brother Coanacochtzin that before they seized him he would first do to them as he had done to their captain'.

MEXICA

In every village they encountered during their approach to Tenochtitlan, the Spaniards inquired about the appearance of the Mexica sovereign, **Moctezuma II**. 'He is a mature man, slender rather than stout, or even thin,' they were informed; 'or not thin but lean, with a fine straight figure'. Any more definitive description was impossible to come by, for his subjects were forbidden – on pain of death – even to gaze on his regal person.

This imperious isolation – and cruelty – was characteristic of the ninth *huey tlatoani*, whose name, appropriately, translates to 'the Lord who Grows Angry'. The accounts of Spanish chroniclers offer a more nuanced perspective. Francisco López de Gómara thought he possessed 'an amiable although severe disposition, affable and well-spoken, and gracious, which made him respected and feared'. He made a similar impression on Alonso de Aguilar, who found him 'very astute, discerning and prudent, learned and capable, but also harsh and irascible, and very firm in his speech'. The individual they encountered, however, was a mere shadow of the ruthless autocrat who had dominated the Valley of Mexico over the 17 years prior to the arrival of the Conquistadors.

Moctezuma II assumed power in 1502 at the age of 34. He had an established pedigree, being the eighth son of the sixth *huey tlatoani* Axayácatl and the grandson of his namesake, the fifth *huey tlatoani* Moctezuma I. He had been inducted into the priesthood of Huitzilopochtli but emerged as a contender for the throne after an elder brother, considered the heir apparent, was killed in a flower war with Huexotzinco. After serving with distinction as commanding general (*tlacochcalcatl*) during Ahuitzotl's final campaigns,

Portrait of Moctezuma II, drawn from contemporary sources by an anonymous artist, and held at the Museo degli Argenti, Palazzo Pitti (Florence, Italy). Francisco López de Gómara described Moctezuma II as 'a man of middling size, thin and like all Indians, of a very dark complexion'. Father Alonso de Aguilar also found him 'of medium height and slender build, with a large head and somewhat flat nostrils'. When not on campaign, the huey tlatoani wore a blue and white mantle *(xiuhtilmahtli)* which no one else could wear, on pain of death. At war, he bore an insignia *(cuahchiahtli)* and two plume tassels *(ananacaztli)* on the side of the royal insignia crest. (Alfredo Dagli Orti/Art Resource, NY)

Xochipilli, the Mexica deity of art, games, beauty, dance, flowers, and song. The indigenous peoples of Mesoamerica struggled to fit the Spaniards into their cosmology. Were they men, gods, or other supernatural beings (*teules*)? Cortés was able to use this uncertainty to his advantage, but he personally never claimed to be anything more than a humble Christian, informing all those he met that, 'We are all mortal and, since our father Adam sinned, we all have to die.' (Museo Nacional de Antropologia, Mexico City – author's collection).

Moctezuma Xocoyotl (the Younger) was the natural choice as successor.

The new *huey tlatoani* made his intentions immediately clear when his first act was to order all of the imperial office holders who had served under his predecessor liquidated. Throughout his reign he was dedicated to purifying the upper echelons of Mexica society by reserving all positions of authority to those of noble blood. No mercy could be looked to when enforcing his law within the Triple Alliance, and he was even more pitiless to his enemies outside it, exterminating entire adult populations in those communities that dared defy him. His rule was one of extremes. While lavish rewards would be bestowed on those who fulfilled his tasks, those who failed risked total annihilation. When his magicians could not explain to his satisfaction the omens of a comet, he had them thrown into prison. When they escaped, he ordered his subordinates 'to kill their wives and all their children, and to destroy their houses,' according to a native account; 'they killed the women by hanging them with ropes, and the children by dashing them to pieces against the walls. Then they tore down the houses and even rooted out their foundations.'

The messianic nature of Moctezuma II and his obsessive dedication to the cold-blooded autocracy he fostered make his total psychological collapse upon the approach of the Conquistadors all the more remarkable. Revisionist historians have sought to find rational justifications for the nature of his relationship with Cortés. They argue that the extravagant gifts Moctezuma II presented to the Conquistadors were intended as a manifestation of his power; that gift giving in Mesoamerica was a tactic by which the giver could raise his status while effectively lowering that of the recipient, if an equal gift could not be returned. A similar rubric is applied to Moctezuma II's welcome when Cortés arrived at Tenochtitlan:

> You have come to satisfy your curiosity about your *altepetl* [city state] of Mexico, you have come to sit upon your throne, which I have kept for you …
> It was said that you would come in order to acquaint yourself with your *altepetl* and sit upon your throne. And now it has come true, you have come. Be doubly welcome, enter the land, go to enjoy your palace; rest your body. May our lords be arrived in the land.

According to recent scholarship, this address must have been delivered in the formal structure of ceremonial speech (*tecpillahtolli*), in which Nahuatl words are heavily laden with reverential language that creates an excessive courtesy in its determination to create no offence. Moctezuma II's assertion he and his ancestors were safeguarding the kingdom only in anticipation of Cortés' arrival was never meant to be taken literally. It was a rhetorical device meant to convey the exact opposite – emphasizing Moctezuma II's heritage and the legitimacy of his reign.

This interpretation is as plausible as it is informed. However, it does nothing to absolve Moctezuma II from responsibility for his own personal downfall, which set in motion the ultimate collapse not just of Mexica hegemony but of all pre-Columbian Mesoamerica.

Whatever his rationale for allowing the Conquistadors into the heart of his empire – to satisfy his curiosity as to whether the interlopers really were supernatural beings (*teules*), to assess their value as ambassadors to previously unknown lands, to win them over against his enemies, or to buy time until he was able to amass sufficient strength against them – once Moctezuma II fell under the spell of Cortés, he could never break free of it. Perhaps the extremes of his rule mirrored the binary nature of his character. In his element, the world of his ancestors, he was absolute master of both himself and his empire. When confronted with a challenge from outside that orderly universe, one that his training and faith could not account for, he swung to the opposite pole of total indecision and fatal irresolution. Within days of his arrival, Cortés had effectively usurped his host, reducing the proud *huey tlatoani* to a mere puppet. Through him the Conquistadors had at their disposal the entire Triple Alliance, which they gorged on like parasites. Mounting Mexica indignation could find no outlet while the paralysis at the top of the social hierarchy persisted. Something had to give. In a final humiliation, Moctezuma II was deposed in favour of his brother, an action unprecedented in Mexica history. He would die betrayed by his guest Cortés, the man to whom he had given everything, and utterly repudiated by his own people.

By the eve of the Spanish conquest, **Cuitláhuac**, *tlatoani* of Iztlapalapa and the eleventh son of Axayácatl, was recognized as the heir to his brother Moctezuma II. As *tlacochcalcatl*, he had led the expeditions that established Cacamatzin on the throne of Texcoco and suppressed a rebellion in the region of Oaxaca. Cuitláhuac was suspicious of the Spaniards from the start, advising Moctezuma II not to allow them entry into Tenochtitlan. Implicated in the conspiracy of Cacamatzin, he had been

Effigy of Cuauhtémoc, last *huey tlatoani* of the Mexica. Bernal Díaz described him as 'a handsome man, both as regards his countenance and his figure … his eye had great expression, both when he assumed an air of majesty or when he looked pleasantly around him'. (Museo del Ejército y Fuerza Aérea, Mexico City – author's collection)

CUAUHTEMOC

arrested and was fortunate to survive the massacre during the festival of Toxcatl. His release was equally providential. When Cortés returned to Tenochtitlan, he demanded his puppet Moctezuma II order the markets be reopened so his men could be provisioned. The *huey tlatoani* despondently replied that his authority had sunk so low he was no longer in a position to give such a command, but that the people might respond to the importuning of one of the lords still held captive in the Palace of Axayácatl. Cortés asked who was best qualified for the task, and when Moctezuma II suggested his brother, Cortés – incredibly – let Cuitláhuac walk out the front gate. Seldom has so great a misjudgement been made so casually, for the two men could not have unleashed a more dangerous enemy. Cuitláhuac immediately assumed the power Moctezuma II had effectively surrendered the day he welcomed Cortés into his city. Finally, the Mexica had a leader prepared to wage total war against the interlopers, and in order to legitimize his standing, Cuitláhuac was recognized as *huey tlatoani*. The pressure he maintained on the besieged Conquistadors gave Cortés no option but to attempt the breakout that came near to total grief on *La Noche Triste*. In the aftermath, Cuitláhuac laboured to restore Tenochtitlan both physically and diplomatically. Had the alliances he sought to forge with Tlaxcala and Michoacán been consummated, Cortés would have been finished, and the peoples of Mesoamerica perhaps free to assert their own destinies. But that stamp of greatness eluded Cuitláhuac. He was formally invested as the tenth *huey tlatoani* on 16 September but was struck down shortly afterwards by the smallpox epidemic then devastating his people.

The very name of **Cuauhtémoc** was an ominous one, for in Nahuatl it means 'Descending Eagle'. Did this anticipate him striking at his enemies like a bird of prey, or did it foreshadow him plummeting to his doom? Although aged only in his early 20s, Cuauhtémoc was an informed choice to succeed his uncle Cuitláhuac as the eleventh *huey tlatoani*. His father was Ahuitzotl, the eighth *huey tlatoani*, while his mother was Tacapantzin, daughter of Moquihuix, the last *tlatoani* of Tlatelolco, who had been slain by Axayácatl when Tenochtitlan forcibly annexed her sister city in 1473. In a time of unprecedented crisis for the Mexica, a leader whose blood mingled that of both royal houses was a critical asset. Tlatelolco not only remained loyal to the Triple Alliance, at the end it was the last redoubt for resistance to the Conquistadors. Raised in Ixcateopan, Cuauhtémoc was marked for greatness when he arrived in Tenochtitlan. Moctezuma II offered him two of his daughters in marriage and kept him close in counsel. Hostile to Cortés from the outset, how he avoided being implicated in the conspiracy of Cacamatzin, and being slaughtered during the festival of Toxcatl, is unknown. But he was prominent in the resistance that ensued; according to one tradition, it was the denunciation of his father-in-law by Cuauhtémoc that prompted the barrage of missiles that struck down Moctezuma II when he attempted to dissuade the Mexica from further violence. His leadership inspired his subjects to continue their increasingly desperate struggle for survival throughout the agony of the long siege, and commanded the respect of the Conquistadors. This availed him little after he finally surrendered, however. Brutally tortured in the futile search for gold, and forced to play the role of puppet ruler previously reserved for the despised Moctezuma II, he was finally executed on the orders of Cortés, who could never fully convince himself such a proud spirit would ever be truly broken.

OPPOSING FORCES

CONQUISTADORS AND ALLIES

The Conquistadors

It is the victors who write the history books, and the established narrative of the Conquest is no exception to this rule. The Conquistadors had two imperatives in establishing what would become the received interpretation of their achievement. First, that it was justified. Second, that it was accomplished against all odds. This account served to inflate their moral, in addition to their martial, superiority. They acted in the service of the Lord and in turn His favour enabled them to strike down the multitudes who defied His will. It was the Spanish David against the Mexica Goliath. 'When in ancient or modern times have such huge enterprises of so few succeeded against so many?' Francisco de Jerez asked in 1534.

In order for this interpretation to be viable, it was necessary for the Conquistadors to downplay the contribution of the native cohorts who sided with them in the bitter and brutal campaign to reduce Tenochtitlan, much to their dismay and that of their descendants. The chronicler of Ixtlilxochitl, *tlatoani* of Texcoco, is at pains to note: 'Since this prince was the greatest and most loyal friend Cortés had in this country, and after God it was with his help and favour that Cortés won, it astonishes me that he did not even tell of Ixtlilxochitl nor of his exploits and great deeds to the writers and historians in order that they would not remain hidden.'

In reality, had it not been for the local peoples flocking to his banner, there is no possibility whatsoever Cortés could have subdued the Mexica after being ejected from their capital on *La Noche Triste*. With no supply chains of their own, the Spaniards were entirely dependent on indigenous logistical support. And even taking into account their vaunted technological superiority on an individual basis, taken as a whole the Conquistadors amounted to no more than one half of 1 per cent of the army that ultimately ground out victory in a protracted war of attrition. 'The Indian empire was in a manner conquered by Indians,' Prescott concedes; 'it would be unjust to the [Mexica] themselves, at least to their military prowess, to regard the Conquest as directly achieved by the Spaniards alone.' Our account will therefore reflect the fact that this was not a conflict between Tenochtitlan and the Conquistadors, but rather between the Mexica Empire on the one hand, and a multinational alliance spearheaded by the Spanish on the other.

Reconstruction of a 16th-century harquebusier, Palace of the Grand Master, Valletta, Malta. Conquistador harquebuses were 1–1.5m long, weighed 8–9kg, and fired a lead ball of up to 140g up to 137m, although it was effective for only about half that distance. They were unmatched in terms of stopping power, but could be outdistanced by Mesoamerican bows, which had a probable maximum range of 180m, and reloading was painfully slow, limiting the harquebus's rate of fire to no more than one round each minute and a half, in comparison to ten or more arrows over the same period. (Author's collection)

This is not to suggest the Spaniards themselves were any less ambitious or aggressive than their reputation suggests. As Cortés assured his compatriots, 'You would conquer the whole land, God giving us health, for Spaniards dare face the greatest peril, consider fighting their glory, and have the habit of winning.' Perhaps the most remarkable feature of his expeditionary force was its autonomy, for Cortés was not a general in command of a professional army, he was a gentleman who arrived at decisions only through the consent of other gentlemen. Throughout the campaign, his leadership had no more foundation than the very fragile status of first among equals that depended entirely upon vision, charisma, and success, and Cortés was tasked on a daily basis with the delicate balancing act of winning over those hostile to his authority without alienating those who considered themselves his friends.

The Spanish capacity for independence of action was a product of the Reconquista, the long struggle with the Moors that was consummated through the conquest of Granada in 1492 by King Ferdinand and Queen Isabella. In pursuit of this ultimate goal, Christian monarchs in the Iberian Peninsula had mobilized their population by arming the citizens and organizing them into militias, a policy contrary to the chivalric code that prevailed throughout the rest of Medieval Europe where warfare was the exclusive preserve of the titled elite. This produced a large pool of skilled and seasoned fighters, all free men and all required to bear arms, regardless of class.

By the beginning of the 16th century, Spain was not only committed to her endemic Crusades against the Moors and Turks but was increasingly drawn into the struggle for supremacy over Italy. In this theatre, where new tactics evolved incorporating flexibility and combined arms, second sons such as Gonzalo Fernández de Córdoba could make both a reputation and a fortune. It was this legacy, which the Spaniards brought with them to the New World, that inflamed the Conquistador spirit.

Because he was able to draw on this Spanish tradition of the citizen militia, Cortés was free to exhibit great flexibility in the disposition of his infantry throughout his campaign in the New World. During the siege of Tenochtitlan, his force was reformed into nine companies of about 50 men each, grouped in turn into three 'divisions', each of three companies. Similarly, throughout the campaign Cortés continually reorganized his cavalry to meet the needs of the moment. At Otumba, he divided his cavalry into squads of five; on the return march to Tenochtitlan from Tlaxcala, he organized his cavalry into four 'squadrons' of ten horses each.

Cortés had with him about 530 European men (mostly Spaniards, but including others with Portuguese, Greek, or Italian ancestry) when he left Cuba. About a quarter of these were *hidalgos* (minor nobles), but the rest were plebeians, and fewer than a third of the total could read and write. Colonists who had struck gold (metaphorical or otherwise) in the Indies generally settled down or returned to Europe. Those who volunteered to test their luck on excursions to the mainland were relatively new arrivals, had not prospered, and lacked high social rank. Contemporary accounts describe the expeditionaries as youthful and impelled by financial imperatives as much as the desire for martial glory. Fernando de Zavallos mentioned in a 1529 lawsuit that the expedition was comprised of young men 'in needy circumstances and easily dominated' by Cortés. Diego de Vargas told an enquiry in 1521 that, 'Among those with Cortés, there were those who said that they were rich, and those who did not have as much as they wished, and there many poor and indebted among them.' This would account for the visceral reaction of the Conquistadors when they gained access to the wealth of Tenochtitlan, as observed by the Mexica: 'They picked up the gold and fingered it like monkeys; they seemed to be transported by joy, as if their hearts were illumined and made new.'

The expedition received spiritual instruction from Father Bartolomé de Olmedo, who would prove an invaluable advisor to Cortés. There were several notaries but only one doctor, Pedro López. A handful of female '*Conquistadoras*' signed on with Cortés who, ignoring Velázquez's prohibition, also embarked several hundred indigenous Cubans, along with Africans, both slaves and freemen (such as Juan Garrido, a former slave who served under Cortés both during the Conquest and later on the expedition to Baja California). Nor was the endeavour limited to human participation. Numerous dogs accompanied their masters on board. These were mastiffs with a taste for human blood that the Spaniards had utilized to great effect as terror weapons in the Caribbean. Their impact on the Mexica – whose only previous experience of canines was the diminutive Chihuahua, which they raised as a source of protein – is vividly captured in a Nahuatl intelligence report on the Conquistadors: 'Their dogs are enormous … their eyes flash fire and shoot off sparks … They are tireless and very powerful. They bound here and there, panting, with their tongues hanging out.' Destined to make an even more decisive impact was a species never before seen on the mainland of the New World. His entire cavalry arm at the outset of his enterprise amounted to just 16 horses, but these would repay Cortés with considerable interest for the expense and painstaking effort required to include them in the expedition, for as he candidly admitted, 'next to God our greatest security was in our horses'.

An assortment of 16th-century firearms, on display in the Palace of the Grand Master, Valletta, Malta. The shock value of these weapons on a preindustrial society far exceeded their actual contribution in battle. Cortés was at pains to drill his harquebusiers when he established quarters in Tenochtitlan. Mexica accounts reflect their awe and dread: 'Each one exploded, crackled, thundered as it disgorged its charge. Smoke spread, suffused, massed over, and darkened the ground. It spread all over, its fetid smell stupefying us, robbing us of our senses.' (Author's collection)

Weapons

Gunpowder weapons have long been perceived as the signature manifestation of European technological superiority. As Oviedo sanctimoniously explained, 'Who can deny that the use of gunpowder against pagans is the burning of incense to Our Lord?' But in practical terms their contribution to the Conquest was actually quite limited. For a start, they were very few in number. More arrived with the ships that landed subsequently, but when Cortés first set foot in the New World, he had no more than 13 harquebusiers

Conquistador mail (right) and horse armour. Mounted Spaniards rode *à la gineta*, with long stirrups, a powerful bit, and a single rein. The legs of the riders would have been pressed back, and the heads of the horses turned by pressure at the neck, not at the mouth. The Mexica struggled to fit the horse within the narrative of their own historical experience, describing them as 'stags' that 'snort and bellow. They sweat a very great deal, the sweat pours from their bodies in streams … They make a loud noise when they run; they make a great din, as if stones were raining on the earth,' and they were adorned with many little bells that made 'a loud clamour, ringing and reverberating'. (Museo del Ejército y Fuerza Aérea, Mexico City – author's collection)

with him, and a modest artillery park under the supervision of Francisco de Orozco. This included 14 muzzle-loading culverins and falconets and probably some breech-loading lombards. These provided critical support in breaking Mexica fortifications during the siege of Tenochtitlan, and, when mounted on board brigantines, in assuring Allied control of Lake Texcoco. The psychological impact of these weapons on a preindustrial culture was significant, but once the Mexica had overcome their initial awe at the novelty and shock value of these weapons, they developed tactics that minimized the threat posed by artillery to their fighters when in contact with the enemy.

In addition, while the Conquistador arsenal was of a different order of technology to the weapons used in the Americas, it came with a corresponding logistical burden that emphasizes just how critical the support of his native

The arrival of the Conquistadors at Vera Cruz, from the 17th-century Conquest of Mexico series. Cortés made a specific point of intimidating Moctezuma II's envoys by putting on a display of horsemanship and demonstrating the firepower of his artillery. The latter, especially, caused consternation when it was reported back in Tenochtitlan: 'A thing like a ball of stone comes out of its entrails: it comes out shooting sparks and raining fire. The smoke that comes out with it has a pestilent odour, like that of rotten mud. This odour penetrates even to the brain and causes the greatest discomfort. If the cannon is aimed against a mountain, the mountain splits and cracks open. If it is aimed against a tree, it shatters the tree into splinters. This is a most unnatural sight, as if the tree had exploded from within.' (Erich Lessing/Art Resource, NY)

allies was for Cortés. He could not have penetrated into the interior of Mesoamerica without it. For example, over the course of one hour in combat during his invasion of Tlaxcala, at one shot per minute per crossbow by the 32 crossbowmen Cortés brought with him, they would have expended 200–350lb of bolts. Similarly, at one shot every one and a half minutes, the 15 harquebuses expended 600 2oz balls and an equal weight of gunpowder, or 130lb, and the four falconets expended 60–200lb in shot per hour. At these rates, the Conquistadors would have burned through a total of 400–700lb of irreplaceable ammunition every hour. With no beasts of burden available, the back-breaking task of manhandling all of these munitions, in addition to the provisions and other baggage, fell entirely on the Totonac bearers who accompanied Cortés from the coast.

European ranged weapons were therefore ancillary to the Conquest. The fate of Tenochtitlan would ultimately be decided at close quarters in hand-to-hand fighting, and the lacunae in Mesoamerican metallurgy that denied the Mexica metal weapons was never more decisive than in this arena. The definitive Mexica weapon, the *macuahuitl*, was a wooden sword edged with serrated obsidian, a volcanic glass that had been flaked into razor sharp blades. In skilled hands these could eviscerate a warhorse, as the Spaniards found out the hard way early in the campaign. But these weapons were only effective against exposed flesh; their impact was severely degraded by body armour, and they could only be utilized in an overhand slashing motion. Time and again, the Spaniards would catch incoming Mexica warriors with quick thrusts of their Toledo steel blades before the enemy could get close enough to deliver a blow. In addition to fighting at a technological disadvantage, the Mexica were further handicapped by the cultural imperatives of their military ethos. They fought to incapacitate, not kill; honour, renown, and promotion were attained through bringing captives back to Tenochtitlan for sacrifice, not leaving them dead on the battlefield. The *macuahuitl* cut clean, but not deep; after each battle, a disproportionate number of Conquistador wounded would live to fight another day.

In the final analysis, the decisive weapon in the Conquistador arsenal was one they brought with them all unwitting, but which would kill more of the people they encountered in the Americas than all of their stratagems and steel combined. As Aguilar put it, 'When the Christians were exhausted from war, God saw fit to send the Indians smallpox.' This was the vanguard of the Eurasian pandemics that would decimate all native resistance, to the point where, in Tenochtitlan, 'the streets were so filled with the dead and sick people that our men walked over nothing but bodies'. Ironically, disease would render the human saga of the Conquest ultimately irrelevant. Whatever their motives, the first representatives of the Old World in the New could not have avoided unleashing the pathogens responsible for a demographic catastrophe on a scale unprecedented in history.

A replica *macuahuitl*. In skilled hands, these weapons could be lethal, as Father Alonso de Aguilar described in his account of an ambush, 'where we found the way barred with intertwined grass ropes'. The Conquistador Cristóbal de Olid and a companion spurred to the attack: 'Since the horses were running with their bell straps, and the artillery had begun firing, the Indians, startled by something so new, hesitated for a moment, so that only two Indians were waiting for the horsemen, one on each side of the road. One Indian at a single stroke cut open the whole neck of Olid's horse, killing the horse. The Indian on the other side slashed at the second horseman and the blow cut through the horse's pastern, whereupon this horse also fell dead.' (Museo Tlatelolco, Mexico City – author's collection)

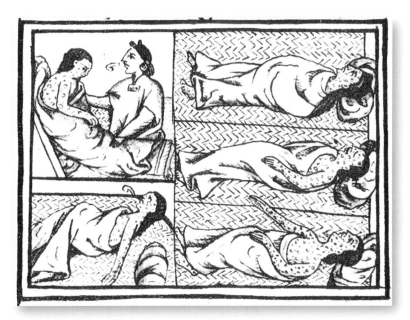

The Allies

However predetermined the impact of disease in the long term, the Spaniards could not have consummated the Conquest in such a short timeframe without the support of those native allies who fought at their side. Throughout the siege of Tenochtitlan, contingents from multiple indigenous kingdoms served alongside – not under – Cortés, wearing plaited garlands of feather-grass on their heads in order to distinguish them from the Mexica, and suffering the heaviest casualties because, as Ixtlilxochitl, the most loyal friend of the Spaniards, put it, 'they were foremost in the fighting'.

The indigenous people of the Americas had no acquired immunity to smallpox, which devastated the continent when it was introduced by the Conquistadors, as illustrated by the *Florentine Codex, c.*1540. In Mexica accounts, 'Sores erupted on our faces, our breasts, our bellies; we were covered with agonizing sores from head to foot. The illness was so dreadful that no one could walk or move. The sick were so utterly helpless that they could only lie on their beds like corpses, unable to move their limbs or even their heads … A great many died from this plague, and many others died of hunger. They could not get up to search for food, and everyone else was too sick to care for them, so they starved to death in their beds.' (*Florentine Codex*, Book XII folio 54/Wikimedia Commons/ Public domain)

Just how important the native contribution to the Conquest was became starkly evident one evening during a subsequent campaign in Pánuco, where an expedition under Jamaica Governor Francisco de Garay had come to grief. As Ixtlilxochitl described it:

> Our people slept that night in an abandoned town where they found the skins of Garay's Spaniards, who had been flayed, and their clothing and arms hung on the walls. This showed clearly that the first Spaniards who came to these parts without native allies had little effect and always had the worst of it. And this was contrary to what happened to Cortés, who wherever he went to subdue or make war against a province always came out winner because he had allies who called the tune and ran the first risks.

Conquest-era military crossbows, like these examples on display in the Palace of the Grand Master, Valletta, Malta, weighed 5.5–6kg and fired wooden bolts with metal heads weighing up to 850g for distances of more than 320m in an arc, or 64m point-blank. (Author's collection)

Because they were the first major confederation in the interior of Mesoamerica to side with Cortés, the role of the Tlaxcala has been writ large. 'The Conquistadors say that the Tlaxcala deserve His Majesty grant them much favour, and that if had not been for them, they would all have been dead,' chronicled Toribo de Benavente Motolinía. Aguilar confirmed that, 'In all the strife and military encounters between the Mexicans and the Christians, the Tlaxcala supported and aided us with all their strength, often risking their very lives for us.'

Political authority in Tlaxcala was divided among four states – Tepeticpac, Quiahuiztlan, Ocotelolco, and Tizatlan – whose lords (*tlatoque*) formed a governing council that had to take into account the interests of the lesser nobility (*tetecuhtin*). Policy – for example, to first war against, and then ally with, the Spanish interlopers – was undertaken after protracted consultation that sought to arrive at a consensus. The commitment to Cortés was realpolitik, not charity, and represented an accommodation, not subjugation. At no stage did the Tlaxcala concede their independence. They refused to participate in any expedition (for example, the sortie against Pánfilo de Narváez) not in their direct interest; they insisted on payment for aid given the Spaniards after *La Noche Triste*; and they returned home immediately after securing their objective, the fall of Tenochtitlan, taking their loot with them.

In addition to the Tlaxcala, other major contributors to the Conquistador cause were the Totonacs, Ixtlilxochitl's city state of Texcoco, and Huexotzinco, whose people boasted of having been more loyal to Cortés than the Tlaxcala, who 'in many places ran away, and often fought badly,' whereas 'we never abandoned or left them … we were the only ones who went along while they conquered and made war here in New Spain,' from Tenochtitlan to Michoacán, Oaxaca, and Guatemala.

The baptism of Ixtlilxochitl, an 18th-century interpretation by José Vivar y Valderrama. The rebel lord of Texcoco accepted the Apostolic faith as Don Fernando Ixtlilxochitl; note Cortés himself standing by as godfather. The personal cost of this defection was high. Many times, while Ixtlilxochitl was fighting alongside the Spaniards in the streets of Tenochtitlan, his relatives would howl at him from the rooftops, condemning him as a traitor to his people, 'in which they in truth were more than right,' his chronicler has to admit. After all his dedication to the Conquistador cause, he was shown no recognition, let alone reward; 'Rather, what was his and his ancestors' was taken from him, and not only this – the houses and the few pieces of land on which his descendants lived were not even left to them.' (Wikimedia Commons/Public domain)

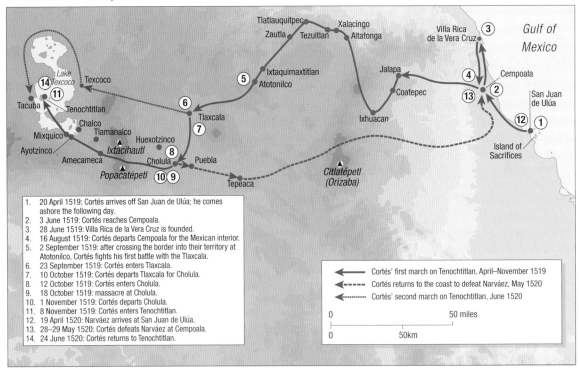

Map legend:
- Cortés' first march on Tenochtitlan, April–November 1519
- Cortés returns to the coast to defeat Narváez, May 1520
- Cortés' second march on Tenochtitlan, June 1520

1. 20 April 1519: Cortés arrives off San Juan de Ulúa; he comes ashore the following day.
2. 3 June 1519: Cortés reaches Cempoala.
3. 28 June 1519: Villa Rica de la Vera Cruz is founded.
4. 16 August 1519: Cortés departs Cempoala for the Mexican interior.
5. 2 September 1519: after crossing the border into their territory at Atotonilco, Cortés fights his first battle with the Tlaxcala.
6. 23 September 1519: Cortés enters Tlaxcala.
7. 10 October 1519: Cortés departs Tlaxcala for Cholula.
8. 12 October 1519: Cortés enters Cholula.
9. 18 October 1519: massacre at Cholula.
10. 1 November 1519: Cortés departs Cholula.
11. 8 November 1519: Cortés enters Tenochtitlan.
12. 19 April 1520: Narváez arrives at San Juan de Ulúa.
13. 28–29 May 1520: Cortés defeats Narváez at Cempoala.
14. 24 June 1520: Cortés returns to Tenochtitlan.

MEXICA

Boys in Mexico were groomed for war from birth. Taking the babe from his mother, the midwife would inform him he 'belongs to the battlefield,' for 'war is thy desert, thy task'. Four days after a male child was born, he was given the symbols of his father's profession. If the father was a warrior, these were a shield and arrows, which were buried with the child's umbilical cord in the direction from which conflict with an enemy was expected.

A jaguar *cuauhxicalli*. The jaguar was the symbol of Tezcatlipoca, the 'Smoking Mirror', one of the most significant gods of the Mexica pantheon. The enemy of Quetzalcoatl, he was arbitrary and cruel, associated with wealth and power, vice and sin. 'He is capricious,' the Mexica believed. 'He mocks us. As he wishes, so he wills. It is as he may want it. He puts us in the palm of his hand. We roll about like pebbles.' It did not escape the attention of the Mexica that Cortés was the physical manifestation of these attributes. (Museo Nacional de Antropologia, Mexico City – author's collection)

The Mexica state existed to enable war. In fact, 'War *was* the empire,' Hassig notes. The compliance of its subjugated peoples depended entirely upon their constantly being made aware of Mexica prowess in battle.

Two separate types of schools offered military training to Mexica youth. The children of the elite would receive instruction at the *calmecac*. From 15 to 20 years of age, commoners would enter the *telpochcalli*, where they would be dedicated to its patron god, Tezcatlipoca, and commence basic training under the war captains (*yaotequihuahqueh*). Each district (*calpolli*) of Tenochtitlan possessed its own *telpochcalli*; there were 20 extant in 1519, providing an education to an average of 419–559 apprentices each.

The House of the Eagle Warriors, headquarters of the elite Mexica fighting unit, located close to the seat of temporal and religious power in the Templo Mayor, Mexico City. (Author's collection)

On his first campaign, a novice warrior's hair was long, signifying that he had not yet taken captives in war. When he took a captive without any assistance, he became a leading youth (*telpochyahqui*) and a captor (*tlamani*), and was introduced to the *huey tlatoani*. For taking three captives, he became a *tiachcauh*, a champion of youths, and resided in the *telpochcalli* to instruct the initiates. For taking four captives, his hair was cut and he was recognized with the title of veteran warrior (*tequihuahqueh*), which entitled him to join the ranks of the two select military orders, the eagles (*cuacuauhtin*) and jaguars (*ocelomeh*). For taking five or six captives, a valiant warrior might be named an elite (*otontin*) warrior, depending on the reputed ferocity of the enemies he had captured. The Huaxtecs, Totonac, and the other coastal peoples were held in low esteem, so for capturing even ten of these a warrior received no acclaim, but if his fifth captive was from Atlixco, Huexotzinco, or Tliliuhquitepec, he gained further honours and was named great captain (*cuauhyahcatl*). Through personal achievement he could rise to the title of general (*tlacateccatl*) and commanding general (*tlacochcalcatl*).

A carving of Mexica warriors. In his anonymous account, one Conquistador admiringly conceded of his enemy that, 'It is one of the most beautiful sights in the world to see them in their battle array because they keep formation wonderfully and are very handsome. Among them are extraordinarily brave men who face death with absolute determination … During combat, they sing and dance and sometimes give the wildest shouts and whistles imaginable, especially when they know they have the advantage.' (Museo Nacional de Antropologia, Mexico City – author's collection)

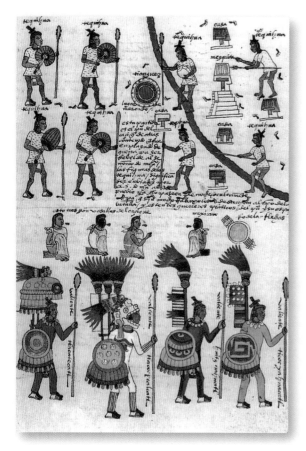

The extremes of rank in the Mexica army are depicted here in the *Codex Mendoza*. The warriors in the upper two files are novices, fitted out in nothing more than plain, unadorned cotton armour. The four figures in the lower file are officers with highly stylized armour. Note the insignia standards (*cuachpantli*), critical to command and control in battle. According to the chronicle of the anonymous Conquistador, these would be 'tied to his back in such a way that it neither hinders him in fighting nor in doing whatever he wishes, and it is so securely bound to his body that it cannot be untied or taken from him unless his body is cut in pieces'. (Wikimedia Commons/Public domain)

Prowess in battle therefore offered the poor a precious opportunity for social advancement. This incentive-based system of promotion did cut both ways, however. As punishment for their poor performance in a flower war against Tlaxcala, Moctezuma II forbade the responsible officers from wearing sandals or entering the imperial palace for a year.

Undistinguished warriors wore a simple breechcloth (*maxtlatl*) and body paint in battle. Only the military leaders wore body armour (*ichcahuipilli*). Officers and valiant warriors wore neckbands of shells or gold, netted capes of twisted maguey fibre and leather corselets, and turquoise earplugs, and they painted their faces with black stripes. The *huey tlatoani* and great lords were adorned in armbands, anklets, and headbands of gold. Only they could wear lip plugs, earplugs, and nose plugs of gold and precious stones; commoners had to make do with wood or bone.

The *huey tlatoani* was the commander-in-chief and often led the army in battle himself. He was accompanied by his closest adviser, the snake woman (*cihuacoatl*), and the four members of his supreme council, the *tlacochcalcatl*, *tlacateccatl*, *ezhuahuancatl*, and *tlillancalqui*. These four offices were filled by the most prestigious nobility, usually by the brothers or other close relatives of the *huey tlatoani*, with the highest in rank reserved for the heir apparent.

In 1519, Tenochtitlan had a permanent military presence estimated in one account at 600 nobles, each accompanied by three or four armed retainers, totalling approximately 3,000 men. Another account cites the much higher figure of 10,000 soldiers stationed in the capital.

The bulk of the army was fleshed out by commoners without military distinction (*yaoquizqueh*). Since most of these were farmers, mobilization was constrained by the agricultural cycle. In the central highlands, planting was done in the spring (usually beginning in late April or May), and harvesting in the late summer or autumn (as late as October or early November). Campaigns therefore ideally would be conducted during the dry season, stretching from around late September through mid-May. Troop movements were also easier during this period, as dirt roads dried out and swollen rivers shrank to fordable streams. Significantly, the Conquistadors arrived well before the festival of Panquetzaliztli, which marked the end of the harvest and signalled the beginning of the campaign season.

Mexica unit organization was determined by the society's base-20 numerical system, which had place values of 1, 20, 400, 8,000, etc. In theory, the army was comprised of *xiquipilli* (units of 8,000 men), mobilized by each city-state under the command of their own *tlatoani*, with the more heavily populated urban centres incorporating subunits from each *calpolli*. Each unit and subunit was designated by a standard (*cuachpantli*), which was mounted on a light bamboo frame strapped to the bearer's back so as not to hinder his fighting. The binding was so tight that it was virtually impossible to take the banner from him without killing him first. While on campaign, experienced warriors were assigned responsibility for up to five novices.

Estimates vary, but during the reign of Moctezuma II, in an ordinary offensive war, from its base population of 200,000 the Triple Alliance could muster 43,000 warriors if every male aged 20 to 50 was called up. For a major campaign, a larger army could be mobilized by calling on commitments from the client states. For the Valley of Mexico as a whole, an army composed of men aged 20–25 would amount to a minimum strength of 54,000; one composed of those aged 20–30 of 105,000.

The ultimate constraints on the Mexica war machine were the institutional limitations of its physical environment. There were no beasts of burden available anywhere in pre-Columbian North America, so the logistical component of a campaign devolved entirely on bearers, who could constitute a full third of the total manpower. Even at this ratio, given every adult male soldier in Mesoamerica consumed, on average, 0.95kg of maize and 1.9l of water per day, an army could have travelled for only eight days on its own supplies, because each bearer carried only 24 man-days of food. Accordingly, prior to every campaign, messengers were dispatched to all client states along the designated route to notify them their tribute obligations were due to support the passing troops. Because 7,600kg of maize, or 330 porter loads, was necessary to feed even a single *xiquipilli* for one day, the burden of subordination to the Triple Alliance was a heavy one.

Effigy of an Eagle Warrior. Members of this unit, along with their counterparts in the Jaguar Warriors, constituted the military elite of the Triple Alliance. Enrolment in their ranks constituted not merely a great honour, but one of the few paths to social advancement available to Mexica commoners. (Museo del Templo Mayor – author's collection)

State of the art Mexica arrowheads, crafted from obsidian. This volcanic glass could be sharpened to produce razor-edge blades that would slice clean through exposed flesh, but their brittleness limited their impact against metal armour. They did still produce a 'splash' effect, however; stone points often shattered on impact against breastplates, spraying fragments into the wearers' eyes, while against mail, reed shafts split on impact, sending slivers through the mesh. (Museo Nacional de Antropologia, Mexico City – author's collection)

Cortés enters Tenochtitlan under the banner of the Virgin Mary in this scene from the *Codex Azcatitlan*. Note the close proximity of La Malinche to the *caudillo*; the prominent status of a Moorish Conquistador (possibly Juan Garrido); and at the rear, bent almost double under the burden of manhandling the supply train, the indigenous bearers. These men were not slaves but specialists called *tlameme*, who were trained from childhood for the role. A typical *tlameme* travelled at a steady jog for 25km a day carrying a load of 22.5kg, and could make journeys as long as 560km. (Wikimedia Commons/ Public domain)

The cost of resistance, of course, was even higher. The Spaniards did not introduce the concept of total war to the Americas. At the conclusion of their campaign against Oztoman and Alahuiztlan, the Mexica had exterminated all of the adults and taken more than 40,000 children for distribution throughout the rest of the empire. The two cities were repopulated by married couples of proven loyalty, including 200 each from Tenochtitlan, Texcoco, and Tacuba. When Tlachquiauhco refused homage, Moctezuma II ordered that no man or woman over 50 was to be spared. When the Mexica took Tututepec, they burned the temple and royal houses and slaughtered the entire population above 9 years of age.

Aztec shields (*yaochimalli*) were of a variety of designs and materials, being constructed from wood, hide, woven cane with a heavy double cotton backing, or plaited palm leaves, decorated with feathers and round plaques of gold. According to the chronicle of the anonymous Conquistador, these shields were 'so strong that only a good crossbow can shoot through them, but arrows do not damage them'. (Museo Nacional de Antropologia, Mexico City – author's collection)

Weapons

The citizens of Tenochtitlan did not bear arms in peacetime. At each of the four entrances to the main ceremonial precinct of Tenochtitlan was an armoury, the *tlacochcalco*, which the Conquistador Andrés de Tapia estimated contained 500 cartloads of weapons.

The Mexica deployed three projectile weapons: spear-throwers (*atlatl*), bows (*tlahuitolli*), and slings (*tematlatl*). The 'darts' used with the *atlatl* were made of oak with feathered butts. Most had fire-hardened tips, while others had obsidian, fishbone, copper, or flint points.

Mexica thrusting spears (*tepoztopilli*) were usually

1.8–2.2m long, with closely set stone blades that formed a nearly continuous cutting edge used for slashing as much as thrusting. Díaz described them as 'lances longer than ours are, with a fathom of blade with many knives set in it, which even when they are driven into a buckler or shield do not come out, in fact they cut like razors so that they can shave their heads with them'.

In close combat, the Mexica employed one-handed and two-handed swords (*macuahuitl*) and clubs, including the *cuahololli*, which had a spherical ball at the business end, the *macuahuitzoctli*, which had a pointed tip and a knob of wood protruding from each of its four sides, and the *huitzauhqai*, which had stone blades.

The Mexica spear-thrower (*atlatl*) allowed for remarkable accuracy and force for up to 46m; experimental tests put the range at over 55m, with an extreme in one test of 74m. The *atlatl* provides almost 60 per cent more thrust, giving it much greater range and accuracy than the unaided spear. *Atlatl*-propelled darts have greater penetrating power than arrows at the same distance. (Museo Nacional de Antropologia, Mexico City – author's collection)

Quilted cotton armour (*ichcahuipilli*) was one-and-a-half to two fingers deep, thick enough to prevent penetration by an arrow or an *atlatl* dart. Elite warriors went into battle decorated in feathers sewn to a backing fabric. Only the nobility was entitled to wear suits of animal skins (*tlahuiztli*), complemented by armbands (*matemecatl*) and greaves (*cozehuatl*) of wood, bark, or very thin gold, covered with leather and feathers.

Tactics

Since there were no horses, Mexica warfare fostered an open formation and an extended line, with the object of enveloping and surrounding an enemy. Signalling was via conch-shell trumpet or drum. Warriors of each unit entered battle shouting the name of their town and beating their shields with their sword.

The best and most experienced warriors initiated the clash between opposing armies in the hope of delivering a decisive blow. Usually the military orders preceded everyone, led by the shock troop *cuahchic* warriors, who fought in pairs and were sworn never to retreat. They also acted as a rearguard if the army was forced to withdraw, and as reinforcements for anyone in difficulty. After the *cuahchicqueh* came the *otontin*, followed by the veteran warriors, the *tequihuahqueh*, who led the first regular units.

In Mexica culture, warfare was as inseparable from religion as life was from death. In the account of Díaz:

> The Mexica never killed our men in battle if they could possibly avoid it, but merely wounded them, so far as to render them incapable of defending themselves, in order that they might take as many of them alive as possible, to have the satisfaction of sacrificing them to their warrior-god Huitzilopochtli, after they had amused themselves by making them dance before him, adorned with feathers.

In a manifestation of this imperative to take an enemy alive, a unique feature of Mexica warfare was the flower war (*xochiyaoyotl*), a ritualized

Effigy of Mictlantecuhtli, the Mexica god of death. The Conquistadors were horrified by such idols, and delighted in destroying them, preferably by pitching them down the sides of the pyramids where they were housed. Father Alonso de Aguilar spoke for the disgust of many when he wrote: 'as a child and youth I began reading many histories and antiquities of the Persians, Greeks, and Romans. I have also read about the rites performed in Portuguese India, and I can truthfully say that in none of these have I heard of such abominable forms of worship as they offered to the Devil in this land. To my manner of thinking there is no other kingdom on earth where such offence and disservice have been rendered Our Lord, or where the Devil has been more honoured and revered.' (Museo del Templo Mayor, Mexico City – author's collection)

campaign against a neighbouring state. By mutual agreement, a date was set for the conflict, which was to be held in a sacred space designated as common ground (the *cuauhtlalli* or *yaotlalli*) and persist for a predetermined period of time. Though bounded by ceremony, these engagements were far from bloodless. The *huey tlatoani* Moctezuma II appointed his younger brother Tlacahuepan responsibility for a 1508 flower war against Huexotzinco, with two more brothers under his command; all three died as the ritual combat spiralled out of control into a very real bloodbath.

Death in a flower war was deemed propitious (*xochimiquiztli*), but its religious overtones notwithstanding, the true purpose of the exercise was to serve Mexica grand strategy. Given its advantage in manpower, by accelerating and intensifying the cycle of these contests, the Triple Alliance could only emerge the victor in what would become a war of attrition. An enemy weakened by this means would be ripe to fall. Moctezuma II had drawn the Tlaxcala into precisely this trap. More than any other factor, it was desperation to escape their inevitable downfall that impelled the Tlaxcala to take the huge risk of forging a partnership with the bearded strangers who entered their midst in 1519.

There is no doubt of Mexica ferocity in combat. Speaking of the desperate, hand-to-hand struggle for Tenochtitlan, Díaz recorded his comrades in arms 'swore over and over again that they had never witnessed such furious fighting, neither in the wars with the king of France, nor even in those with the grand Turk himself'. The Conquistadors, however, were unimpressed by Mexica command and control during battle. In one of his letters to Charles V, Cortés described them as being 'so many that they got in each other's way, and could neither fight nor run'. Antonio de Solís y Rivadeneyra, too, noted Mexica officers 'could scarce govern their men; for, when they came to engage, they were directed either by fear or rage, as is usual among such multitudes, being equally eager to attack, and to run away'. However, it should be remembered the Spaniards only came to blows with the Mexica after Alvarado had pre-emptively massacred the flower of their military elite. It would have been hard for them to compensate for this decimation of their most prestigious and experienced warriors.

Nevertheless, a remarkable feature of the Conquest is the extent to which the Mexica did adapt to the unprecedented circumstances in which they found themselves. For example, their accounts describe how they evolved tactics to counteract the firepower of Cortés' gunpowder weapons:

> When the [Mexica] discovered that the shots from the harquebuses and cannons always flew in a straight line, they no longer ran away in the line of fire. They ran to the right or left or in zigzags, not in front of the guns. If they saw that a cannon was about to be fired and they could not escape by running, they threw themselves to the ground and lay flat until the shot had passed over them. The warriors also took cover among the houses, darting into the spaces between them.

The Mexica had no taboos against utilizing Spanish weapons against their erstwhile owners. In his narrative, Ixtlixochitl recalled how he defeated a Mexica general who carried a Spanish lance liberated from a Conquistador he had killed. Ixtlilxochitl 'dealt him three blows with a war club, the last of which struck him in the head and took off half of it, including one ear. When the enemy saw their general dead, they took such courage and attacked our people so impetuously that they made them retire toward the courtyard.'

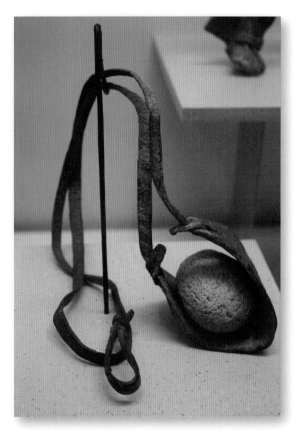

The Mexica used maguey-fibre slings (*tematlatl*) to hurl stones at the enemy. The missiles thrown by the slings were not casually collected at the battle site but were hand-shaped, rounded stones stockpiled in advance, and these also were sent to Tenochtitlan as tribute. Comparative data indicates such slings had a range in excess of 200m. (Museo Nacional de Antropologia, Mexico City – author's collection)

Other Mexica improvised lances by lashing captured swords to poles, or experimented with utilizing crossbows after captives had been forced to show them how the mechanisms functioned.

Most importantly, the Mexica understood the constrained nature of urban warfare enabled them to minimize the great advantage the Spaniards enjoyed in open country, the strike power of their cavalry. Ixtlilxochitl noted that during the siege of Tenochtitlan, the Mexica 'prepared themselves very well and thoroughly beforehand, throwing many stones in squares and streets so that the horses could not run on them and resorting to many other stratagems of war'. In their own account, the Mexica recalled:

> Some of our warriors stationed themselves on the rooftops of the Quecholan district, which is near the entrance to the market place, and from there they hurled stones and fired arrows at the enemy. Others broke holes in the rear walls of all the houses of Quecholan, holes just big enough for a man's body to pass through. When the cavalry attacked and were about to spear our warriors, or trample them, or cut off their retreat, they slipped through the holes and the mounted men could not follow.

Fighting the decisive battle of the campaign in their own capital, therefore, represented a necessary evil for the Mexica. They could not hope to defeat the Spaniards in open battle, not with so many allies flocking to the Christian banner. Their one prospect of victory lay in drawing their enemies into the metropolis and bleeding them, street by street, until either the Conquistadors lost heart and abandoned the venture or their allies deserted or turned on them.

Tenochtitlan, 1520–21

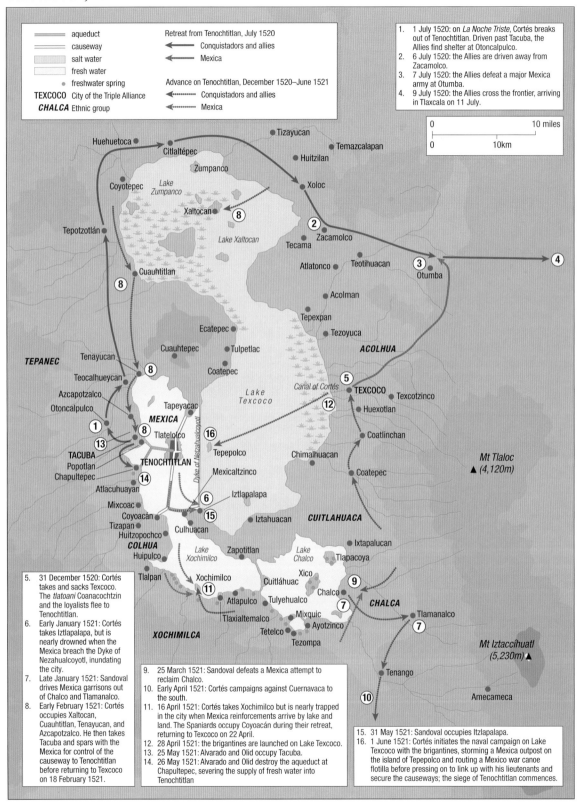

Legend:
- aqueduct
- causeway
- salt water
- fresh water
- freshwater spring
- **TEXCOCO** City of the Triple Alliance
- **CHALCA** Ethnic group

Retreat from Tenochtitlan, July 1520
- ⟵ Conquistadors and allies
- ⟵ Mexica

Advance on Tenochtitlan, December 1520–June 1521
- ⟵⋯ Conquistadors and allies
- ⟵⋯ Mexica

1. 1 July 1520: on *La Noche Triste*, Cortés breaks out of Tenochtitlan. Driven past Tacuba, the Allies find shelter at Otoncalpulco.
2. 6 July 1520: the Allies are driven away from Zacamolco.
3. 7 July 1520: the Allies defeat a major Mexica army at Otumba.
4. 9 July 1520: the Allies cross the frontier, arriving in Tlaxcala on 11 July.

0 ———— 10 miles
0 ———— 10km

5. 31 December 1520: Cortés takes and sacks Texcoco. The *tlatoani* Coanacochtzin and the loyalists flee to Tenochtitlan.
6. Early January 1521: Cortés takes Iztlapalapa, but is nearly drowned when the Mexica breach the Dyke of Nezahualcoyotl, inundating the city.
7. Late January 1521: Sandoval drives Mexica garrisons out of Chalco and Tlamanalco.
8. Early February 1521: Cortés occupies Xaltocan, Cuauhtitlan, Tenayucan, and Azcapotzalco. He then takes Tacuba and spars with the Mexica for control of the causeway to Tenochtitlan before returning to Texcoco on 18 February 1521.

9. 25 March 1521: Sandoval defeats a Mexica attempt to reclaim Chalco.
10. Early April 1521: Cortés campaigns against Cuernavaca to the south.
11. 16 April 1521: Cortés takes Xochimilco but is nearly trapped in the city when Mexica reinforcements arrive by lake and land. The Spaniards occupy Coyoacán during their retreat, returning to Texcoco on 22 April.
12. 28 April 1521: the brigantines are launched on Lake Texcoco.
13. 25 May 1521: Alvarado and Olid occupy Tacuba.
14. 26 May 1521: Alvarado and Olid destroy the aqueduct at Chapultepec, severing the supply of fresh water into Tenochtitlan

15. 31 May 1521: Sandoval occupies Itzlapalapa.
16. 1 June 1521: Cortés initiates the naval campaign on Lake Texcoco with the brigantines, storming a Mexica outpost on the island of Tepepolco and routing a Mexica war canoe flotilla before pressing on to link up with his lieutenants and secure the causeways; the siege of Tenochtitlan commences.

THE CAMPAIGN

THE FIRST BATTLE OF TENOCHTITLAN

Moctezuma II arrived to greet Cortés in full pomp, borne on a litter, and accompanied by the highest-ranking lords of the Triple Alliance, including Cuitláhuac, Cacamatzin, Totoquihuatzin (the *tlatoani* of Tacuba), and Itzquauhtzin (the governor, or *cuauhtlatoani*, of Tlatelolco). The first greetings were oddly low-key, given the tableau. 'Are you Moctezuma?' Cortés asked. 'Yes, I am he,' the *huey tlatoani* replied. The two men exchanged gifts. Then Moctezuma II invited his guests to take up residence in the palace of his father, the *huey tlatoani* Axayácatl, where he joined them that evening. The exact content and actual intent of the address he then made to Cortés has been bitterly contested ever since, because in many ways it represents the crux of the entire Conquest.

'Our lord, you must be tired, you have experienced fatigue, but you have arrived at your city,' Moctezuma II began. This was mere court formality. But Cortés, writing ten months later to Charles V, asserted Moctezuma II went much further: 'Thou hast come to govern the great city of Mexico. Thou hast come to descend upon thy mat, upon thy seat, which for a moment I have guarded for thee.' According to Cortés, his host had recognized in

The site where Cortés encountered Moctezuma II is commemorated with this memorial in modern Mexico City. On that fateful day, both men stepped down from their conveyance – the *caudillo* from his horse, the *huey tlatoani* from his litter – and met face to face. The act of lèse-majesté Cortés then committed should have sent an immediate signal to Moctezuma II that his guest had no respect for his authority, customs, or person: 'I stepped forward to embrace him, but the two lords who were with him stopped me with their hands so that I should not touch him.' Those two lords – presumably Cacamatzin and Cuitláhuac – must have subsequently harboured bitter regret that they did not do more than restrain Cortés at that moment. (Fabioj/Wikimedia Commons/CC-BY-SA-3.0)

Mexica human sacrifice, depicted in the *Codex Magliabechiano*. 'In the time it would take one to make the sign of the cross he thrusts the knife into the victim's chest and opens it, and takes out the heart while it is still hot and beating,' one anonymous Conquistador remarked. Another Spaniard to have witnessed such ritual butchery, Father Alonso de Aguilar, admitted: 'I was spellbound with wonder and terror.' (Biblioteca Nazionale Centrale, Florence, Italy/ Bridgeman Images)

the Conquistadors incarnations of the venerated forefather who had led the ancestors of the Mexica to Tenochtitlan, only to be repudiated and pass into exile: 'And we have always held that those who descended from him would one day come back … and take us as vassals.'

Beneath the fine rhetoric, this speech in fact reflected indecision, not submission. Moctezuma II was still trying to sound out who or what Cortés actually was. But Cortés was only too happy to interpret it literally. He had intuited the fatal irresolution of his host, which he would viciously exploit. But for the meantime, he was content to issue disingenuously vague platitudes of satisfaction with the hospitality he had received.

The Spaniards were free to spend the next few days experiencing the wonders of Tenochtitlan; the great marketplace, the ballcourts, the imperial zoo, the botanical gardens. But there was horror, inextricably meshed with the splendour, gruesome evidence everywhere of the death cult that defined Mexica religious life, from endless tiers of skulls to priests wearing the flayed skins of their victims. When Moctezuma II personally introduced Cortés to the idol of Huitzilopochtli in the temple atop the Great Pyramid (*teocalli*), the hearts of captives who had been sacrificed earlier that day were still smouldering in braziers. 'Every wall of this chapel and the whole floor had become almost black with human blood,' a disgusted Díaz recalled, 'and the stench was abominable'.

This period of relative accord ended abruptly when the Tlaxcala brought alarming news from the coast: Juan de Escalante, Cortés' lieutenant at Villa Rica, and six other Spaniards, with many Totonacs, had been killed. Qualpopoca, Moctezuma's regional representative at Nauhtla, had demanded the usual half-yearly tributes from the Totonacs, who, newly emboldened by their alliance with Cortés, had refused to pay. Escalante, insisting the Totonacs were under Spanish protection, had been drawn into the fray, setting off with a force of up to 50 Spaniards (including two horsemen, two cannon, three crossbows, and two harquebuses), and 8,000–10,000 Totonacs. He succeeded in burning Nauhtla, but after the Totonacs were subsequently routed, he was forced to withdraw, in the process suffering a mortal wound and leaving behind one of his company, Juan de Argüello. Qualpopoca had this captive sacrificed and dispatched his head, complete with black curly beard, to his sovereign in Tenochtitlan.

Pedro de Ircio assumed temporary command at Villa Rica, but the implications of the defeat were significant. All of Mesoamerica now had definitive proof the Spaniards were neither immortal nor invincible: 'After this overthrow, the belief that the Spaniards were *teules* (supernatural beings) had altogether vanished,' Díaz noted. The Totonacs were wavering; if they defected back to the Triple Alliance, Villa Rica would fall, cutting Cortés off from the Gulf.

Cortés could not risk leaving Tenochtitlan, but neither could he ignore this reversal, so he exercised the only available option. On 14 November – less than a week after making his acquaintance – Cortés sought an audience with Moctezuma II in his chambers. As usual, he was accompanied by his senior captains (Alvarado, Sandoval, Velázquez de León, Lugo, and Ávila), but on this occasion, he brought at least two dozen more men, all heavily armed.

Cortés brushed off the usual pleasantries and got straight to the point, accusing Moctezuma II of complicity in the affair at Nauhtla. The *huey tlatoani* denied any responsibility and immediately proposed an inquiry into what had happened, promising the guilty would be punished. Cortés wasn't satisfied. He delivered a blunt ultimatum: Moctezuma II must immediately accompany him back to the Palace of Axayácatl, where he would be placed under Spanish supervision: 'Everything will be forgiven, provided you now come quietly with us to our quarters, and make no protest. You will be as well served and attended there as in your own palace. But if you cry out, or raise any commotion, you will immediately be killed by these captains of mine, whom I have brought for this sole purpose.'

Moctezuma II utterly capitulated. Informing his guards, advisers, and relatives the god Huitzilopochtli had told him that it would be good for his health to live a while with the newcomers, he mounted his litter and was borne by his own nobles into Spanish captivity.

The proud Moctezuma II was now the passive puppet of the Conquistadors. When Mexica agents returned from the coast with Qualpopoca, his sons, and 15 other Mexica officers, he handed them over to Cortés, who had them staked out on a pile of wooden bows, arrows and swords taken from the armoury of the palace and burned alive. Cortés made sure Moctezuma II himself was taken to witness the spectacle, adding the precaution of chaining him in irons to 'prevent an uproar' among the throngs of assembled Mexica, who observed this (to them) completely novel form of execution – and abject humiliation of their *huey tlatoani* – in complete silence.

Having subjected Moctezuma II to this disgrace, Cortés, ever the dissembling manipulator, personally released him from his chains. Offering soothing apologies for the necessity of his bondage, Cortés suggested he could now return to his own palace if he wished.

Statue of Coatlicue, the Mexica goddess who gave birth to the moon and stars, and was the mother of Huitzilopochtli, the god of the sun and war, patron god of Tenochtitlan. Not all of the indigenous peoples who encountered the Spaniards were conflicted over their status as human or divine. When the Conquistadors marched inland from Villa Rica, they were accompanied by a captain of the Totonac warriors, Teuche, a veteran of conflict with the Mexica. 'I know that you and your companions are men and not gods,' he told Cortés; 'that you hunger and thirst and weary as men.' He prophesized that the Spaniards would ultimately be overwhelmed in Tenochtitlan, for 'one hundred thousand men will fight you now, and when these are dead or vanquished, that many again will come forward, and again and again by the hundred thousand … But if you determine to die, then I shall go with you.' (Museo Nacional de Antropologia, Mexico City – author's collection)

Note: the illustration covers a base area of 5.7km x 4.7km

MEXICA
1. Between 3,000 and 10,000 garrison troops
2. *c.*30,000 reserves

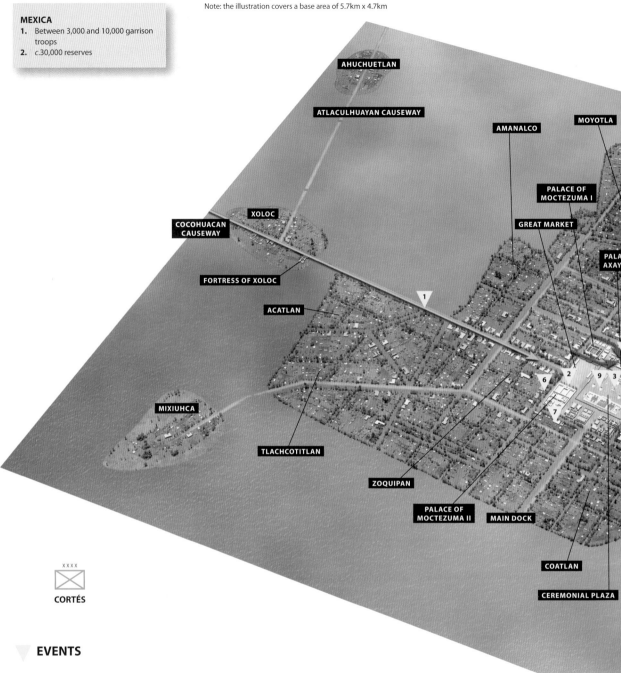

AHUCHUETLAN

ATLACULHUAYAN CAUSEWAY

MOYOTLA

AMANALCO

PALACE OF MOCTEZUMA I

XOLOC

GREAT MARKET

COCOHUACAN CAUSEWAY

PALAC AXAYÁ

FORTRESS OF XOLOC

ACATLAN

MIXIUHCA

TLACHCOTITLAN

ZOQUIPAN

PALACE OF MOCTEZUMA II

MAIN DOCK

COATLAN

CEREMONIAL PLAZA

xxxx
CORTÉS

▼ EVENTS

1. 8 November 1519: Cortés enters Tenochtitlan and encounters Moctezuma II, who houses his guest in the Palace of Axayácatl.

2. 14 November 1519: Cortés seizes Moctezuma II.

3. 16 May 1520: in the absence of Cortés, who has departed for the coast in order to confront a punitive expedition under Pánfilo de Narváez, his deputy Pedro de Alvarado massacres the Mexica nobility during the Festival of Toxcatl in the Ceremonial Plaza.

4. 24 June 1520: Cortés returns to Tenochtitlan.

5 25 June 1520: Cortés releases Cuitláhuac, who assumes power as acting *huey tlatoani* in Tenochtitlan. The Mexica rise up against Cortés and commence laying siege to the Palace of Axayácatl.

6 26 June 1520: de León takes the Palace of Moctezuma II; unable to hold this prize, he withdraws to the Palace of Axayácatl.

7. 27 June 1520: trying to placate his erstwhile subjects, Moctezuma II is repudiated and wounded by a barrage of missiles.

8. 28 June 1520: the allies make a failed attempt to break out of Tenochtitlan.

9. 29 June 1520: Cortés takes the Temple of Yopico; unable to hold it, he withdraws to the Palace of Axayácatl.

10. 30 June 1520: the death of Moctezuma II. The allies again attempt to break out of Tenochtitlan.

11. 1 July 1520: *La Noche Triste* (Night of Sorrow): trapped on the westerly causeway to Tacuba, the allies suffer horrific losses fighting their way through fanatical Mexica resistance.

THE CONQUISTADOR ARRIVAL IN TENOCHTITLAN, 1519–20

Hernan Cortés and the allies arrived in Tenochtitlan on 8 November 1519, entering the city via one of its causeways. Although Moctezuma II was initially welcoming, the relationship quickly turned sour. In June the following year, the Mexica rose up in revolt against their Spanish overlords. Cortés was able to break out of the city, but at a terrible cost.

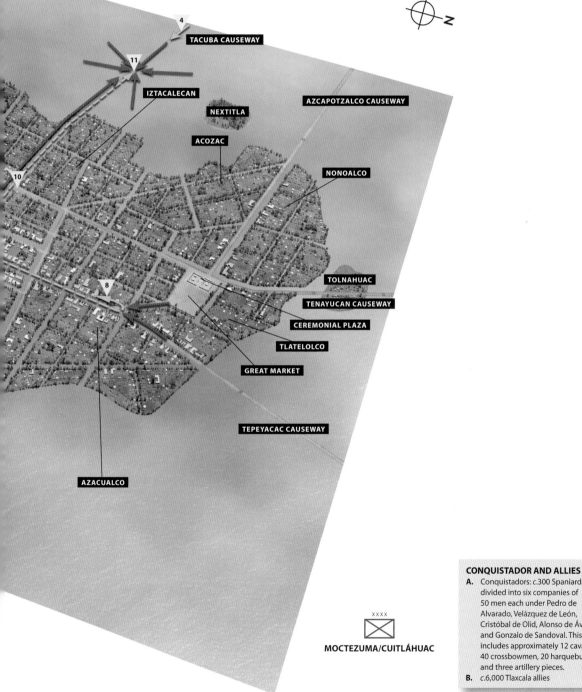

4

TACUBA CAUSEWAY

11

IZTACALECAN

NEXTITLA

AZCAPOTZALCO CAUSEWAY

ACOZAC

NONOALCO

10

8

TOLNAHUAC

TENAYUCAN CAUSEWAY

CEREMONIAL PLAZA

TLATELOLCO

GREAT MARKET

TEPEYACAC CAUSEWAY

AZACUALCO

xxxx

MOCTEZUMA/CUITLÁHUAC

CONQUISTADOR AND ALLIES

A. Conquistadors: c.300 Spaniards divided into six companies of 50 men each under Pedro de Alvarado, Velázquez de León, Cristóbal de Olid, Alonso de Ávila, and Gonzalo de Sandoval. This includes approximately 12 cavalry, 40 crossbowmen, 20 harquebusiers, and three artillery pieces.

B. c.6,000 Tlaxcala allies

Three Mexica warriors. On the far left is an Eagle Knight; according to the anonymous Conquistador, the Eagle Knight heads were 'of wood covered on the outside with feathers or incrustations of gold and precious stones, and are something wonderful to see'. (*Florentine Codex*, page IX, F, 5v/Wikimedia Commons/ Public domain)

This was doubtless a ruse, but Moctezuma II's response is indicative of the extent to which his overriding priority from the moment the aliens entered his kingdom was retaining his own title and position. He thanked Cortés for the generous offer of his liberty, but politely declared his intention to remain in the house of his father. His motivation was fear. If he was released, the city would be free to rise up against the interlopers in a blaze of war Moctezuma II no longer had the heart to wage. If he failed to lead his people in such a struggle, the hot-blooded lords of his household, many of whom he knew were chafing at the daily insults they were being subjected to by this handful of arrogant outsiders, would find a new *huey tlatoani* who would. A broken man, Moctezuma II now preferred the shadow of authority under Spanish auspices over the demands – and concomitant risks – of wielding actual power.

It was an incredible gamble, but through this decisive assertion of his authority, Cortés both reassured his allies (on learning what had happened, the Totonacs resumed supplying Villa Rica) and assumed effective control over Tenochtitlan. For the next five months, Moctezuma II played out his role as the model collaborator. Enraptured in what modern clinicians would diagnose as Stockholm Syndrome, he spent countless hours entertaining Cortés, inviting him on hunting excursions in the surrounding countryside and to matches of the Mesoamerican ball game (*tlachtli*). In return, Cortés had a novel surprise in store for his host.

Always determined to cover any contingency, Cortés, aware the Mexica could cut him off from the mainland at a moment's notice by raising the bridges on the causeways, determined to construct a new fleet capable of evacuating his men (and the considerable store of treasure they had accumulated) via the lake. Placing Martin López of Seville in charge of construction, he sent to Villa Rica for spare parts salvaged from the ships scuttled at the coast. The result was enough to rig four brigantines, whose sails and their harnessing of the wind – techniques unknown to Mesoamerican culture – fascinated Moctezuma II when he accompanied Cortés on an excursion.

Increasingly sure of his position, Cortés began dispatching scouting parties to reconnoitre the outlying districts of the empire and report back on their estimated value, especially in terms of gold production. Gonzalo de Umbria was assigned the Mixtec region of Zacatula (modern Oaxaca); Diego de Ordaz headed north to Coatzacoalco on the Gulf of Mexico; while Andrés de Tapia and Diego Pizarro inspected the mines of Pánuco.

All seemed calm, but passions were roiling just below the surface. Cacamatzin, *tlatoani* of Texcoco, now bitterly regretted advising Moctezuma II to welcome Cortés into Tenochtitlan. Mortified by the docile subservience of his uncle, he emerged as the ringleader of a cabal amongst the Mexica elite determined to rise up against the Spaniards. Numbered amongst those drawn into the circle of plotters were the *tlatoani* of major cities, including Iztlapalapa (Moctezuma II's brother Cuitláhuac), Coyohuacan, Tacuba, and Matlatzinco. However, the conspiracy was betrayed to Moctezuma II,

CONQVISTA DE MEXICO POR CORTES...

who immediately informed Cortés. Acting through his regal mouthpiece, the *caudillo* ('strong leader') ordered all those suspected of involvement arrested and incarcerated in Tenochtitlan, replacing Cacamatzin as *tlatoani* of Texcoco with one of his sons, Cuicuitzcatl.

Emboldened, Cortés moved to consolidate his authority. He had Moctezuma II swear formal submission to King Charles V (enabling the Conquistador to establish a legal framework by which any future resistance from the Mexica would represent treason and an act of rebellion), took possession of all the imperial treasuries, and had the temple atop the Great Pyramid purged and converted into a church, the idols of the Mexica gods being replaced by Christian effigies of St Christopher and the Virgin Mary.

Cortés seemed to have settled into playing the role of puppet master. But a new threat loomed on the horizon. Word of Cortés' achievements – and rumours of the wealth he was in the process of amassing – had filtered back to Cuba. Smallpox had arrived in the island shortly after Cortés left, so Velázquez had his hands full, and given another expedition to the mainland could not sail before the first favourable winds of the following spring, the lieutenant governor was forced to spend the winter fuming at his erstwhile subordinate's treachery. This did, however, afford him ample time to mobilize an enormous punitive expedition, ultimately comprised of 19 ships, more than 800 soldiers (twice the size of Cortés' original force), 20 cannons, 80 harquebusiers, 120 crossbowmen, and 80 cavalry (over four times as many horses as Cortés had brought). This left Cuba on 5 March under the command of Pánfilo de Narváez, who had orders to dispose of Cortés and assume control in Tenochtitlan. Having retraced Cortés' route from Cozumel, he

This scene of the struggle for Tenochtitlan, part of the 17th-century Conquest of Mexico series, is idealized and anachronistic, but it does emphasize the significance of the causeways to the campaign. Without a secure grip over these key chokepoints, Cortés could not hope to take the city. Asserting, and maintaining, such authority in turn hinged on whether he could first seize control of the lake. The siege was therefore a combined arms operation, land and naval units acting collaboratively towards the ultimate goal. (Private Collection/Bridgeman Images)

arrived off San Juan de Ulúa on 19 April. The Totonacs defected to Narváez, who also initiated a dialogue with Moctezuma II, making sure to inform the *huey tlatoani* that Cortés, far from being the personal representative of King Charles V, was nothing more than a freebooting renegade.

Cortés was in a dangerous position. He had only 200 men with him in Tenochtitlan. Two of his lieutenants – Velázquez de León in Coatzacoalco and Rodrigo Rangel in Ghinantla – were scouring the interior for gold with about 130 men each, and there were a further 100 with Sandoval, who had been appointed governor of Villa Rica. But this was a challenge he could not ignore. Cortés set out for the coast at the beginning of May with just 80 or so men, leaving Alvarado in command of 120 Spaniards and the Tlaxcala to maintain order in Tenochtitlan.

He had dispatched instructions to both of his outlying contingents to join him at Cholula, which they did (a major relief to Cortés, given León was not only a kinsman of Diego Velázquez but a brother-in-law of Narváez). He was less successful with a message asking the Tlaxcala for 4,000 men; they had no desire to become embroiled in an internecine Spanish conflict.

After some derisory attempts at negotiation, entered into with bad faith on both sides, Cortés pushed on via Orizaba to Tanpaniguita, about 40km from Cempoala, where Narváez had advanced his banner. Having been reinforced by the arrival of Sandoval and about 60 men from Villa Rica (which still left him outnumbered more than 2:1), Cortés made preparations for a general assault. He arranged his men in five companies. His cousin Diego Pizarro was given command of 60 men and tasked with seizing Narváez's artillery. Sandoval, with 80 men, including Tapia, was to take Narváez himself, dead or alive. León, with 60 Conquistadors, and Ordaz, with 100 more, would target Narváez's key lieutenants. Cortés took personal charge of the reserve. The mercenary nature of the Spaniards, on both sides, was never more evident. Cortés promised 1,000 castellanos to the first man to lay his hands on Narváez, 600 to the second, 400 to the third, and 200 to the fourth. Narváez was more direct, pledging 2,000 pesos to whoever killed Cortés. More constructively, León slipped 1,000 pesos to Narváez's gunmaster, Rodrigo Martínez, to stop up the touchholes of Narváez's cannon with wax.

On the evening of 28 May, under cover of darkness and the pouring rain, Cortés struck. He was inside Cempoala before Narváez could react. Sandoval's detachment clambered up the steps of the main pyramid and stormed the temple at its summit, where Narváez had established his headquarters. Narváez, his right eye gouged out in the struggle, was forced to submit when Martin López, serving under Sandoval, set fire to the thatched roof of the temple. After Narváez was dragged into captivity, his bare feet burned and blistered, most of the fight went out of his army; the last holdouts, clustered atop another pyramid, surrendered after Cortés turned their own artillery against them.

It was a complete triumph, nearly bloodless and almost laughably easy. Cortés had lost just two men, while 15 of Narváez's company were killed (among them Diego Velázquez, the young nephew of Cuba's lieutenant governor). 'Indeed, general, you have reason to be proud of this victory, and of my being taken prisoner,' Narváez haughtily asserted. 'I am every way thankful to God for it, and likewise for the brave companions he has given me,' Cortés replied, 'but I can assure you that this victory is the least brilliant we have yet gained in New Spain.' He could well afford to indulge in such condescension, for the men Narváez had brought with him now deserted en-masse, bringing the total under Cortés' command to more than 1,300 rank and file, 96 horses, 80 crossbowmen, and 80 harquebusiers. Narváez would remain incarcerated at Villa Rica; his officers and about 40 other loyalists who refused to defect were dispatched as prisoners to Tenochtitlan on foot, escorted by a handful of Cortés' men.

Once again, Cortés' instinct to go for the jugular had paid off in spectacular fashion. He had never been in a stronger position. In fact, he felt confident enough to divide his forces, sending León with 120 men (including 100 of Narváez's) to settle the coast beyond the Pánuco River, and Ordaz with another 120 men (again including 100 of Narváez's army) to establish a colony in Coatzacoalco. Cortés was only too happy to take possession of Narváez's fleet, too; after unloading the provisions and equipment at Villa Rica, he scuttled all but two ships, having first stripped them of their sails, masts, hardware, rigging, navigation equipment, and everything else he could store against any possible future contingency. The two remaining vessels would serve as transports, shuttling back to the Caribbean for domestic brood stock, including mares, goats, calves, sheep, and even chickens.

But it was at this moment of apparent triumph that an urgent message arrived from Tenochtitlan. The city was up in arms, and everything Cortés had accomplished hung in the balance.

At the time, it must have seemed like a minor detail for Cortés, who was preparing to march out against Narváez, when Moctezuma II asked for permission to stage an annual religious festival dubbed the Feast of Toxcatl. Cortés offhandedly granted it, as did his deputy Alvarado some days later, albeit with the proviso that there be no human sacrifices.

Staged at the height of the dry season, the Feast of Toxcatl was a supplication for the life-giving rain, second only to blood in its significance for the circle of life. 'This was the most important of their fiestas,' Sahagun explained many years later. 'It was like our Easter and fell at almost the same time.' But as preparations for the festival advanced, the Spaniards became

Cortés referred to Tenochtitlan as 'the City of Dreams', exclaiming that it was without question 'the most beautiful thing in the world'. At its heart was the Temple Complex, depicted here in a scale model in the Museo Nacional de Antropologia, Mexico City. The plaza is dominated by the Templo Mayor, in front of which is the rectangular *tzompantli*, the rack displaying tens of thousands of skulls harvested from sacrificial victims. In front of that is the circular temple dedicated to Quetzalcoatl. On the right is the Temple of Yopico, which the Conquistadors stormed shortly before evacuating the city on *La Noche Triste*. (Author's collection)

The Spaniards (and their Tlaxcala allies) desperately fight to keep the Mexica at bay from the Palace of Axayácatl in this scene from the murals of Diego Rivera in the Palacio Nacional, Mexico City. Complementing their incessant assaults during the day, the Mexica employed psychological warfare at night. When evening fell, the Spaniards trapped within the walls would serve as unwilling witnesses to spectral and diabolical visions; human heads jumping of their own accord, severed limbs marching, decapitated corpses rolling and groaning. (Author's collection)

increasingly uneasy. Their Tlaxcala allies were reporting rumours of insurrection. The Mexica had stopped provisioning them with food. It was Cholula all over again.

On the fourth day of the festival, Alvarado decided to act. Leaving 60 men at the palace, he led the other half of his force, plus the Tlaxcala, to the Temple Complex. After posting harquebusiers atop the walls enclosing the patio, where the elaborate Serpent Dance was to commence, the Spaniards sealed off all the entrances; the Eagle Gate, the Gate of the Canestalk, and the Gate of the Serpent Mirror.

Oblivious, the hundreds of Mexica within the patio, the political and military elite of the Triple Alliance, were swept up in the cathartic frenzy of the ritual, dancing to the shrill piping of flutes and the rhythmic pounding of drums. Swords drawn, the Spaniards filed in among the dancers, forcing their way to the musicians. They singled out the lead drummer, and cut off his arms. Then they cut off his head, which rolled across the floor. This was the signal for a general massacre. The Spaniards attacked all the celebrants, butchering them without mercy. Most of those assembled were cut down where they stood. Some attempted to force their way out, but the Spaniards murdered them at the gates. Others sought to scale the walls, or fled to the communal houses, or lay down among the victims and feigned death. But the Spaniards were relentless, hunting down all those who tried to escape. 'They ran everywhere and searched everywhere; they invaded every room, hunting and killing,' according to the *Florentine Codex*. 'The blood of the warriors flowed like water and gathered into pools. The pools widened, and the stench of blood and entrails filled the air.' Meanwhile, the men Alvarado posted behind at the palace slaughtered almost all of the lords arrested on suspicion of conspiring against Moctezuma II, including his nephew Cacamatzin (who

With the Conquistadors trapped in the Palace of Axayácatl by the enraged Mexica, Moctezuma II was ordered to address his people in a bid to restore calm. The heartsick *huey tlatoani* was in no mood to take orders from the *caudillo*: 'I neither wish to live, nor to listen to him, for to such a pass have I come because of him.' He was cajoled into making the effort, but his erstwhile subjects responded with a barrage of missiles, as depicted in this print from the 17th-century Conquest of Mexico series. It was 'as if the sky was raining stones, arrows, darts and sticks,' recalled Father Alonso de Aguilar. According to Bernal Díaz, Moctezuma II was struck by 'an arrow, and three stones from a sling, by which he was wounded in the arm, leg, and in his head'. Grievously injured, he was led below. He would not depart the Palace of Axayácatl alive. (Erich Lessing/Art Resource, NY)

fought so fiercely he had to be stabbed 47 times). The hapless *huey tlatoani* could do nothing more than watch while they, and his own household and attendant nobility, were butchered.

As word of the slaughter spread, all of Tenochtitlan recoiled, first in horror, then in rage. The drums began to sound the alarm, an ominous, throbbing beat. Warriors hastened to the armouries at each of the four entrances to the temple precinct, where they snatched up weapons and descended, in ever thickening numbers, on the Spaniards. Alvarado had initially been entirely satisfied with his handiwork among the dancers in the patio; 'He who begins the battle, wins,' he had boasted to a fellow Conquistador. Now he had to fight his way back to the Palace of Axayácatl, taking a sling stone to his face in the process. Covered with blood from his wound, he had the effrontery to tell Moctezuma II, 'See what your people have done to me.' A broken man, the *huey tlatoani* could only reply, 'Alvarado, if you had not begun it, my men would not have done this. You have ruined yourselves and me also.'

The palace was now under siege; enraged Mexica were at the doors and swarming over the walls. Even with Spanish cannon wreaking havoc in their packed ranks, it was only a matter of time before they broke in. Alvarado put a knife to Moctezuma II's heart and told him to order his warriors to back off. He went to the roof and did his best to persuade his people their struggle was in vain. Itzquauhtzin, the governor of Tlatelolco, also spoke: 'Let battle be abandoned. Let the arrow and shield be stilled … your lord says, "may battle cease," for they have placed his feet in irons.' This joint appeal apparently had some effect, for the siege abated, the citizens of Tenochtitlan retiring to recover and mourn their dead. It was Moctezuma II's last service to the Spaniards, and it cost him the final dregs, not just of his dignity, but his authority, too. For the Mexica, as well as the Conquistadors, realized subsequently that Vázquez de Tapia was right when he said that, had the *huey tlatoani* not done as he was asked, Alvarado and all of his men would have been killed that day.

Alvarado doubtless felt his best option was to strike first. But the consequences of the massacre, Díaz dryly noted, 'were certainly different to what he had expected, and bad became worse'. He had, however, struck a deep wound in the heart of Mexica society. So much of Tenochtitlan's military elite had been eliminated at a stroke – generals, great captains, renowned warriors – it was now an open question whether the armies of the Triple Alliance, for all their numbers, could recover their cutting edge in time to meet the unprecedented challenge in their midst.

Cortés, meanwhile, was on his way. Having left a garrison at Villa Rica, he linked up at Tlaxcala with the two colonizing expeditions he had dispatched, bringing his force up to nearly 1,200, and recruited a sizable number – perhaps as many as 2,000 – Tlaxcala auxiliaries.

Marching by way of Texcoco, Cortés took his expedition round the north side of the lake in order to approach Tenochtitlan from the west via the shortest causeway at Tacuba. Local *tlatoani* urged him to call a halt in a city on the mainland and send for Alvarado and Moctezuma II to join him, arguing that would give him much greater freedom of action than being trapped in the metropolis on the lake. This was intelligent tactical advice, but Cortés was thinking in terms of grand strategy. If he failed to enter Tenochtitlan, he would effectively concede the city to the rebels. He was determined to assert the authority he had invested so much in imposing, and reclaim everything that was his. Accordingly, he marched into the capital on 24 June, unopposed, to sullen silence.

This larger Spanish force now occupied the nearby Temple of Tezcatlipoca in addition to the Palace of Axayácatl. But if Cortés thought he could bluff his way into restoring order, he was gravely mistaken. With the noose tightening around him, he made a fatal error; as a gesture of goodwill, he released Cuitláhuac. The brother of the *huey tlatoani* immediately took command of the resistance, giving it the legitimacy and leadership the Mexica had craved during the long, disgraceful months of Moctezuma II's collaboration.

Too late, Cortés realized he had to secure a line of retreat. He ordered Ordaz to fight his way back to the mainland with 300 men, including cavalry, harquebusiers, and most of the crossbowmen. This party made little progress before it was subjected to a fusillade of stones hurled from the rooftops. A handful of Spaniards were killed and nearly all the rest, including Ordaz, wounded. Keeping up a hail of missile fire, the Mexica drove the Conquistadors back to the Palace of Axayácatl, setting fire to it and punching a breach in the wall. With no water to spare, the Spaniards had to smother the flames with earth and whatever other material they could scavenge. Desperate fighting left more Spaniards wounded, including Cortés himself; the Mexica were only repulsed because the narrow opening at the breach made them easy prey for cannon and small-arms fire.

Cortés' worst fears had been realized; he was trapped, unable to reach the causeways, and the Mexica had burned his brigantines, so there could be no escape via the lake. The Mexica were relentless in their assaults, while Spanish sorties to secure the neighbouring buildings – even a successful sally to capture Moctezuma II's palace – were futile because they lacked the manpower to hold such exposed positions. Every excursion ended with the Spaniards retreating back to the palace, dragging their many wounded with them, and leaving one or two dead behind. Cortés could not win this war of attrition; food supplies were dwindling, and the only available water was brackish and unhealthy from wells hastily dug in the courtyard, which was subjected to an incessant barrage of stones hurled from the surrounding rooftops.

Ever resourceful – or increasingly desperate – Cortés ordered the construction of wooden siege machines, which could shelter 20–25 men, including harquebusiers and crossbowmen, giving them portable cover to take the fight outside. He also sought to see if Moctezuma II might yet be able to salvage something from the situation. But the *huey tlatoani* was no longer the Conquistadors' trump card. On the evening of 27 June, he dutifully ascended to the roof of the palace, covered by the shields of two Spaniards. Eyewitness reports of what happened next contradict each other completely. Cortés, in his letter to King Charles V, related that Moctezuma II was hit by the first stone before he could get a word out. According to other observers, there was a moment of silence among the Mexica at the sight of their erstwhile lord, until he began his appeal to them, which was swiftly cut off. In the account of the *Codex Ramirez*, it was the hot-blooded Cuauhtémoc who incited his comrades by mockingly demanding to know what was being said by his uncle, that 'whore of the Spaniards'. Díaz, however, reported that after the usual courtesies, the Mexica captains coldly informed Moctezuma II they had elected Cuitláhuac in his stead (an act without

Nezahualcoyotl (1402–72), ruler of Texcoco, as depicted in the 16th-century *Codex Ixtlilxochitl*, accoutred for war in a feather tunic and kilt (*ehuatl*) worn over padded cotton armour (*ichcahuipilli*), greaves (*cozehuatl*), armbands (*matemecatl*), wristlets (*matzopetztli*), sandals (*cactli*), a helmet, and a gold lip plug. He is armed with a feather-fringed shield (*yaochimalli*) and a sword (*macuahuitl*) and carries a small upright drum (*huehuetl*) on his back to signal the attack. (Wikimedia Commons/ Public domain)

precedent in Mexica history) and had sworn not to stop fighting until all the alien intruders were wiped out. In any case, Moctezuma II's speech, or attempt at it, attracted a barrage of missiles. Grievously injured, the erstwhile *huey tlatoani* was led below.

Cortés was running out of options. At dawn, he led his war machines out of the palace, supported by crossbowmen, harquebusiers, and four cannon, hauled by the Tlaxcala, in a bid to fight his way through to one of the causeways. But even this concentrated firepower could not overcome the sheer weight of Mexica numbers. The following day, Cortés turned his attention to the Temple of Yopico in the adjacent sacred precinct. Its heights enabled the Mexica to overlook and enfilade his position. The war machines succeeded in getting the Spaniards to the base of the pyramid before they were totally destroyed. Cortés had the satisfaction of battling all the way up the steps, burning the temple, and hurling its idols (and their priests) down the steep slopes. But again, there was no way he could hold the prize he had taken, and he had no choice but to retreat back to the palace, leaving more irreplaceable dead scattered in his wake.

It was obvious there could be no more half measures. Cortés, who had sworn he would 'sooner be cut to pieces than leave the city,' now accepted there was no alternative. Everything had to be staked on the entire Spanish force breaking out. They would succeed or die.

Whatever else happened, Moctezuma II would not be accompanying them. The conventional account maintains that he expired, from his wounds and despair, on the morning of 30 June. However, it is equally likely he was disposed of by his Conquistador friends. Mexica accounts claim that, after the Spaniards had been driven from the city, Moctezuma II was found dead with his feet in chains and five dagger wounds in his chest. If so, this was scant

BATTLE FOR THE TEMPLE OF YOPICO, TENOCHTITLAN, 29 JUNE 1520 (PP. 58–59)

Trapped inside Tenochtitlan when the city rose against him, an increasingly desperate Cortés resorted to cannibalizing the interior of the Palace of Axayácatl for timber with which to build rudimentary war machines. Borne by his Tlaxcala allies, these miniature siege towers, or two-storey, wooden tanks, each sheltered 20 or 25 men, including harquebusiers and crossbowmen, offering them mobile cover with which to project their firepower. When these proved incapable of forcing passage to one of the causeways out of the city, Cortés turned his attention to a more proximate threat.

The Temple of Yopico, atop a pyramid in the ceremonial plaza directly adjacent to the palace on its eastern side, had been occupied and fortified by the Mexica, who were using it as a lookout to keep track of Conquistador movements within the palace and direct movements against them.

On 29 June, Cortés led a detachment under Pedro de Villalobos and spearheaded by his war machines against the temple. The Conquistadors had to fight their way through file after file of Mexica warriors in the streets to reach the pyramid. In the process, the war machines were bombarded with stones from the rooftops of every house en route. As a result, they were practically destroyed by the time they reached the foot of the pyramid. But they had served their task; and a rearguard of Conquistadors, alongside the allies, could still utilize their frames to form a perimeter (**1**) and keep the masses of Mexica warriors congregating in the plaza (**2**) at bay.

Cortés was now free to lead his best fighters up the near vertiginous 100 steps of the pyramid to the temple at the summit.

The Mexica fought them all the way with every weapon at their disposal; shooting arrows and slinging stones, casting spears and *atlatl* darts, thrusting with pikes, and fighting hand to hand. Some deliberately hurled themselves into the approaching Conquistadors in a bid to knock them off their feet.

Cortés (**3**), leading from the front beneath his personal banner (**4**) and that of Spain (**5**), had his shield tied to his left arm, his left hand having been bandaged from a wound incurred during a sortie the previous day.

Even while fighting continues to rage on the steps and the terraces, the Conquistadors at the summit have set fire to the temple (**6**), from which smoke is starting to billow. Some Spaniards have hurled the stone idol of Xipe Totec, the hideous Mexica flayed god, down the steps (**7**). Others are flinging the Mexica priests after them (**8**); 'like black ants they tumbled down,' as one eyewitness put it.

This operation was a complete tactical success, but at the strategic level it amounted to nothing. Cortés could not hold this exposed position, not with overwhelming numbers of Mexica, responding to the beat of the signal drums throbbing from atop the Templo Mayor (**9**), swarming into the plaza. The Spaniards had no option other than to retreat back into the palace, leaving behind approximately 20 irreplaceable dead. Few of the survivors emerged unscathed; 'What a fight it was,' marveled Bernal Díaz; 'it was certainly something to see our men all running with blood and covered with wounds.' Overall, as another participant in the desperate struggle, González Ponce de León, concluded, 'It was not the day to be in bed.'

reward. Whatever the case, Cortés did not scruple to dispose of the remaining *tlatoani* in his possession, including Itzquauhtzin and the *tlacatectal*, Atlixcatzin, who as a son of the former *huey tlatoani* Ahuitzotl may have been the most likely candidate to succeed Moctezuma II.

Having made the decision to escape, Cortés now had to determine what route to take. Tlaxcala was the ultimate objective, but striking directly east across Lake Texcoco was out of the question; even if the

A Mexica canoe. These vessels, hewn from a single tree trunk, ranged in size from this smaller model to the large bulk transports, 15m or more in length, capable of carrying either 60 passengers or 3 tonnes of maize. The tens of thousands of canoes at their disposal enabled the Mexica to project force anywhere around the perimeter of Lake Texcoco, as the Spaniards found out, to their cost, on *La Noche Triste*. Only through construction of the brigantines was Cortés able to nullify this challenge. (Museo Nacional de Antropologia, Mexico City – author's collection)

Spaniards could somehow commandeer enough canoes, this would require abandoning all the horses (and probably the cannon as well) before crossing at least 15km of open water while being subject to pursuit and interdiction by the Mexica.

The northern causeway to the mainland, via Tepeyacac, offered the fastest overland road to Tlaxcala. But the Spaniards could expect the Mexica also to have appreciated this, meaning it would be the most tightly secured, and in any case, accessing it required the longest march through Tenochtitlan. The southern causeway crossed the deepest water of the lake and exited through Coyoacán and Iztlapalapa, hostile cities that would prove major obstacles. Although Cortés might have anticipated aid once he reached Chalca territory, he would also have been more vulnerable to attack from causeways and canoes in the densely populated southern end of the valley. In addition, the land rose much more sharply from the lakes in that direction. A column making its way east would be funnelled into narrow, easily choked trails as it clambered into the heights, and Cortés wanted to put Tenochtitlan behind him as fast as possible.

That left the western causeway, through which Cortés had returned to the capital just days earlier. Its terminus was Tacuba, a founding partner of the Triple Alliance and hence a large, hostile city, but accessing it required the shortest march inside Tenochtitlan, offering the best chance of the breakout going undetected, and, since it led away from Tlaxcala, it was possible the Mexica would have left it relatively unguarded.

With the route decided, the next priority was organization. Aware that the Mexica had removed the spans crossing the canals, Cortés ordered the palace itself to be cannibalized, stripping the walls and ceiling beams for timber in order to construct a portable bridge. Four hundred Tlaxcala and 150 Spaniards, under the command of Francisco Rodriguez Magariño, would be responsible for transporting it and spanning each gap in the causeway. Another 250 Tlaxcala and 50 Spaniards were assigned to haul the artillery.

Sandoval, Ordaz, Francisco Acevedo, Antonio de Quiñones, Tapia, and Lugo led the vanguard, comprised of the best 100 men Cortés had available, tasked with clearing the streets ahead of the main body. Cortés followed with the bulk of the army, Avila and Olid being in positions of tactical command. Close behind them was Cristóbal de Guzmán, Cortés' major-domo, responsible for the treasure, which by this point, after six months of systematic looting of the Triple Alliance, amounted to an astounding 8 tons of gold, silver, and gemstones. Next in line came the rest of the Tlaxcala, guarding those prisoners who had not yet been liquidated, including Chimalpopoca, the son of Moctezuma II, and two daughters of the late *huey tlatoani*. Finally, the rearguard, commanded by León and Alvarado, consisted of the main body of the cavalry and the greater part of Narváez's troops. In the confusion, word had not reached the balance of the latter, holding their posts at the Temple of Tezcatlipoca, that the evacuation was underway. They were left behind to a grisly fate.

Cortés set off at midnight, taking advantage of mist and light rain. He succeeded in bridging the first three canals – the Tecpantzinco, the Tzapotlan and the Atenchicalco – without being detected, a remarkable achievement given the column must have snaked many hundreds of metres through the city, and could not have been moving quickly or silently, even with the horses' hooves muffled. It wasn't until it reached the fourth canal, the Mixcoatechialtitlan, that the escape was discovered.

The Mexica, who had nearly let their quarry slip away, were roused by the shrill calls of conch shells and the rumbling beat of drums. Their canoes now filled the lake, descending on the causeway from both sides and subjecting the retreating Conquistadors to a withering crossfire of missiles. Those at the head of the column had to run the Mexica gauntlet and were forced to swim across the last two gaps in the causeway. But the vanguard, and then Cortés and his companions in the second division, succeeded in reaching the mainland. Cortés took five horsemen (including Olid and Sandoval) and rode to assist those left behind, only to arrive at a scene of complete chaos.

For all their significance, the cavalry and ranged weapons specialists were only a small minority of the Spaniards serving under Cortés. The backbone of the Conquistador force was the infantry, sword and buckler men accoutred like these replicas in the Palace of the Grand Master, Valletta, Malta. Few of them emerged from the saga of the Conquest with material gains in any way commensurate with their risks and sacrifices, however. 'I say that the least of the Conquistadors merited being highly rewarded, since at their own expense and effort they gave the king this large new world,' Father Alonso de Aguilar stated. But although 'the least of all these men was greatly deserving, yet most of them were impoverished'. (Author's collection)

The bulk of the column, already losing formation and on the verge of panic, had approached the gap of the Toltec canal when, Díaz bitterly noted, 'as misfortunes never come singly, it happened that two of our horses should slide out on the wet planks, become unmanageable, and roll over into the lake. This caused the bridge itself to overbalance,' and it too crashed into the water. Sensing vulnerability, the Mexica began pouring onto the causeway at this point; although the Spaniards were able to keep them at bay, they were unable to recover the bridge. 'As, however, those behind kept continually pushing on those in front, the opening in the canal was speedily filled up with dead horses and their riders,' Díaz continued. Mexica accounts confirm, 'The canal was soon choked with the bodies of men and horses, they filled the gap in the causeway with their own drowned bodies. Those who followed crossed to the other side by walking on the corpses.'

Men, horses, treasure, and cannon were all lost, drowned or trodden underfoot. The only instinct was self-preservation; many years later, one eyewitness sourly recalled that, 'no one at the moment was interested in anything except saving his own skin'. Cortés, seeking to rally his shattered command, only succeeded in tumbling into the lake, where he was swiftly surrounded by vengeful Mexica warriors. He would have been borne off for triumphant sacrifice had it not been for the timely intervention of Cristóbal de Olea and Antonio de Quiñones.

The situation was worst at the tail of the column. In the confusion, Alvarado's horse was killed. He was able to make a fighting retreat on foot (though not, as legend would have it, by vaulting over the breach in the causeway) and cut his way back to Cortés, bringing only seven Spaniards and eight Tlaxcala with him, all soaked in blood. When his commander demanded to know what had happened to the rest of the rearguard, Alvarado replied: 'Señor, all of them are here and if some are not, forget them.' Indeed, most of those bringing up the rear of the column were never seen again. Many, unable or unwilling to contest the breaches, fell back to their quarters at the Palace of Axayácatl. There they held out for a day or two before being overwhelmed, dragged to the apex of the Great Pyramid, and sacrificed to satisfy the insatiable bloodlust of the Mexica gods they had done so much to provoke.

The lost city of Teotihuacan, the cultural and commercial centre that dominated Mesoamerica prior to the rise of the Triple Alliance. At its height, this metropolis would have been the only one in pre-Columbian America that could have rivalled Tenochtitlan for size and splendour, but when Cortés passed by in 1520 during the desperate retreat after *La Noche Triste,* it was in ruins, its great pyramids abandoned and overgrown. (Author's collection)

It was indeed, as the Spanish chroniclers dubbed it, *La Noche Triste*, the night of tragedy. The precise death toll will never be known, but Martin Vázquez was probably right when he testified in 1525 that 600 Spaniards were killed or taken. The number of Tlaxcala lost is even more speculative, but it must have run into the thousands. Among the dead were some of Cortés' most valued subordinates, including Velázquez de León; key native allies, such as Xiuhtototzin, governor of Teotihuacan, who had taken the side of the pretender Ixtlilxochitl in the war for the throne of Texcoco; and his most prized hostage, Chimalpopoca, the son of Moctezuma II.

Yet, while the retreat had degenerated into a tactical disaster for Cortés, his strategic position had improved. He had escaped the death trap of Tenochtitlan, and most of the men who survived were his own veterans; it was no coincidence that the bulk of those who had arrived with Narváez were placed at the rear of the column, or even left behind. Cortés still had a solid core of reliable lieutenants, including Alvarado, Olid, Sandoval, Tapia, Ordaz, and Ávila. He still had Doña Marina. And when he was assured his shipbuilder, Martin López, was still alive, he immediately replied, 'Well, let's go, for we lack nothing' ('*Vamos, que nada nos falta*').

Cortés was already mapping out his return to Tenochtitlan, but such bravado could not disguise the parlous condition of his company at that moment. The effective number of Spaniards under his command had been cut at least in half, and few of the beleaguered remnant had escaped without wounds; his Tlaxcala allies had been decimated; all of his cannon were lost, along with most of his gunpowder; the immense treasure of the

THE SPANISH CAVALRY BREAKS THE MEXICA LINE, THE BATTLE OF OTUMBA, 14 JULY 1520 (PP. 64–65)

Having lost half their number fighting their way out of Tenochtitlan, the few hundred Conquistador survivors and their remaining Tlaxcala allies, half-starved, exhausted, almost all of them wounded, spent the next several days on the run in a desperate bid to make it back to Tlaxcala territory and safety. They were intercepted near the village of Otumba by a Mexica army mobilized to finish off the alien menace once and for all.

Caught on the march, the Spanish and Tlaxcala infantry formed up back to back, creating a hollow rectangle (**1**), the two long sides facing outwards, with those too wounded or ill to fight clustered in the middle. A female Conquistador, Maria de Estrada, was prominent in the front ranks, wielding a pike. The Spaniards' dogs, too, great armoured war hounds (**2**), savagely defended their masters, snarling and snapping as they burst into the Mexica front lines.

But the Mexica 'came on so fearlessly that they surrounded us on two sides,' Bernal Díaz recalled: 'We dared not to charge them … lest they should break up our formation … any soldier who left the ranks to follow some of the Indian captains and swordsmen was at once wounded and ran great danger.' The air was thick with arrows, spears, sling stones and *atlatl* darts pouring from all directions into the tightly pressed Conquistador ranks, while Mexica warriors were free to launch assaults in successive waves to exploit any opportunity (**3**). After hours of fighting, surrounded and massively outnumbered, the Spanish position was growing desperate. 'We could resist but feebly,' Cortés himself admitted in his report to Charles V, 'since we were tired and nearly all of us wounded and fainting from hunger.'

Cortés had one trump card left to play. He realized the Mexica general, Tenochtitlan's high priest the *cihuacoatl*, was coordinating his men via a system of signal banners (**4**) from atop his litter. Leaving Diego de Ordaz in command of the infantry, Cortés took five horsemen – Gonzalo de Sandoval (**5**), Cristóbal de Olid (**6**), Alonso de Avila (**7**), Pedro de Alvarado (**8**), and Juan de Salamanca (**9**) – and broke through the Mexica line. When they reached the *cihuacoatl*, they slaughtered him, his litter bearers (**10**), and his senior officers (**11**). It was Cortés himself (**12**) who knocked the *cihuacoatl* (**13**) from his litter to the ground, where Salamanca ran him through with his lance.

The loss of both their command structure and their signal system threw the Mexica ranks into confusion, allowing Cortés and the remnant of his army to escape.

Triple Alliance – so painstakingly accumulated – was sinking into the mud at the bottom of Lake Texcoco; and only two dozen battered, limping horses remained, none able to raise more than a trot.

The Spaniards had to move. At dawn, the bedraggled remnants of the column reached Popotlan, near Tacuba, but Mexica skirmishers forced them past the city. After fording three rivers (the Tepzolatl, Tepzolac, and Acueco), Cortés was finally able to call a halt in Otoncalpulco, where the temple patio was surrounded by a wooden palisade.

Burdened by their wounded and subjected to incessant sniping by the Mexica, it took the Spaniards all of the following day to march the 8km to Teocalhueycan, which stood atop a rounded hill, and was protected by a barrier of rocks. Fortunately, the people of the town were Tepanecs, no friends of the Mexica. So the retreat continued, step after agonizing step, as the column shuffled east. The Spaniards spent the following two nights at Tepotzotlan and then Citlaltépec, the populations of both lakeside towns fleeing upon their approach. They reached Xoloc the next night, but fierce resistance drove them back from Zacamolco the following day. More and more men, unable to sustain the pace, were succumbing to the wounds they had incurred on *La Noche Triste* or in subsequent Mexica ambushes. Bypassing the legendary lost city of Teotihuacan, when the Conquistadors arrived at Otumba, just as the trail began to climb towards the northernmost pass over the mountains towards Tlaxcala, they found the plains swarming with tens of thousands of Mexica warriors; Cuitláhuac had determined to finish the alien threat here, once and for all. Outnumbered, exhausted, and on the brink of annihilation, only a desperate cavalry charge, led in person by Cortés, enabled the Spaniards to struggle free and push on to Xaltepec, where they could see the frontier. On 9 July, ten agonizing days after *La Noche Triste*, Cortés crossed back into Tlaxcala territory.

THE SECOND BATTLE OF TENOCHTITLAN

The Spaniards were safe, but the cost was high; since *La Noche Triste*, Diaz recorded, 'including the battle of Otumba, we lost in killed, and those who were taken prisoners, above 870 of our troops, and above 1,200 Tlaxcala'. The losses were not exclusive to those under Cortés' direct command. While passing through Tlaxcala on his way to Tenochtitlan after defeating Narváez, Cortés had ordered the 16,000 pesos worth of gold with him be transported back to Villa Rica under the guard of Juan de Alcántara. He now learned that after this party had departed for the coast with five horses, about 50 foot soldiers, and 200 Tlaxcala porters, it had been wiped out at Calpulalpan, the Mexica absconding with the coffers full of treasure. Cortés also received confirmation the party of Narváez's loyalists he had dispatched under escort to Tenochtitlan from Villa Rica, another 50 men at least, had disappeared after being ambushed in Quechula, a tributary of Tepeaca. 'Our whole strength now merely consisted in 440 men, 20 horses, 12 crossbows, and seven harquebuses,' Díaz lamented.

Cortés, therefore, had every reason to be grateful to his hosts for the sanctuary they offered. As his chief smelter of metals, Antonio de Benavides, later testified, had it not been for the Tlaxcala, 'no Spaniard would have escaped the Mexica because there was nowhere else to go'. But the fact

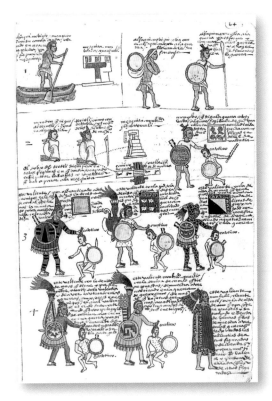

Note that the warriors in this scene from the *Codex Mendoza* have seized their enemies by the hair, a gesture of submission. The Mexica propensity to take prisoners in battle, as opposed to killing their enemies outright on the battlefield, has been interpreted as a critical inherent weakness in their mode of warfare. However, it differed little from accepted practice in Europe, where prisoners were taken to be ransomed afterwards. The Mexica model was actually more decisive, for in addition to its propaganda effect, ritualized sacrifice eliminated a potential threat entirely, whereas selling a captive back to your foe only guaranteed you would meet him again some other day. (Wikimedia Commons/Public domain)

the Conquistadors had suffered a major defeat could not be disguised. Envoys arrived from Tenochtitlan urging the Tlaxcala to abandon the partnership they had forged with the outsiders, who had no respect for the gods all peoples of Mesoamerica held in common. If they turned on their impious guests, Cuitláhuac was prepared to offer the Tlaxcala equal stakes within an expanded Triple Alliance.

Xicotencatl the Younger, who had never become reconciled to Cortés, argued fervently for accepting this proposal. The Tlaxcala nation – and the fate of the Conquistadors – balanced on a knife edge. But it was the voices of the previous generation that ultimately held sway in council. Xicotencatl the Elder and Maxixcatl, old men who had spent their entire lives at war with the Mexica, could not accept any accommodation with the hereditary enemy even now. The envoys from Cuitláhuac returned to Tenochtitlan empty-handed.

On the other hand, if Cortés thought the Tlaxcala were acting on his behalf out of good will, he was swiftly disabused. In exchange for their continued support, they demanded the right to exact tribute from Cholula, Huexotzinco, and Tepeyacac (all previously subordinate to the Mexica), command of a fortress to be built in Tenochtitlan, an equal division of the spoils looted from any towns or provinces conquered, and perpetual freedom from tribute themselves. In no position to argue, Cortés conceded every point.

The Spaniards remained in Tlaxcala for 20 days. Many of them, nursing wounds and grievances, petitioned Cortés to return home. But the *caudillo* was adamant in his determination to press forward. Retreat would invite disaster; 'to show the natives, especially those who are allies, that we lack courage would turn them against us the sooner'. The only guarantee of safety was victory; after all, 'Fortune always favours the brave.' As to numbers, 'Victories are not won by the many but by the valiant.' Accordingly, on 1 August, Cortés led a column consisting of 420 Spaniards, 17 horses, six crossbowmen (but no cannons or harquebuses, the gunpowder being exhausted) and 2,000 Tlaxcala allies in a punitive expedition against Tepeaca. This hilltop fortress lay astride the best route between Tenochtitlan and the sea at Villa Rica, and was the centre of tribute for the Triple Alliance in the flat region stretching from the volcano of Popocatépetl to the slopes of Mt Orizaba. Aside from its strategic benefits, a quick victory here would boost morale within the depleted Conquistador ranks, impress potential allies, and intimidate those contemplating resistance.

After taking Tepeaca on 7 August, Cortés used the city (which he renamed Segura de la Frontera) as his base while he set about pacifying the surrounding provinces. Over the balance of that summer, all the towns of the region either offered their submission, like Huexotzinco and Cuetlaxtlán, or, like Quechula, Izúcar, Tecamachalco, and Acapetlahuacan, were sacked, their male populations liquidated, the women and children branded and sold into slavery. This was done, Cortés later explained, so 'as to strike fear into the [Mexica] and also because there are so many people there that if I did not impose a great and cruel punishment they would never be reformed'. As always, the *caudillo* was careful to retain the choicest booty for his own purposes. Prior to distributing the human spoils of the campaign, he made sure the finest of the indigenous females were secretly set apart, 'so that when it came to a division among us soldiers, we found none left but old and ugly women,' Díaz bitterly recollected.

Little assistance was forthcoming to their tributaries by the Mexica, who were focused on repairing and fortifying their capital, readying it for the next encounter with the Spaniards they knew must come. Cuitláhuac did make one proactive attempt to block further Spanish expansion by sending troops south of Cholula to Cuauhquecholan and Itzyocan, straddling the main pass into the Valley of Mexico. But this force was driven out of both towns by an Allied army comprised of 200 Spanish infantry, 13 horsemen, and 30,000 indigenous levies, securing for Cortés control over the gateway to Lake Texcoco.

Rebuffed by the Tlaxcala, Cuitláhuac did reach out to the only other great power in Mesoamerica that could tip the balance of power as an ally – the Tarascan empire of Michoacán. Messengers were posted to the court of their *cazonci* (monarch), Zuangua, in his capital of Tzintzuntzan. The Mexica envoys spoke enthusiastically of their prospects in battle with the Spaniards should the two empires join forces: 'Why should we not be successful, since everyone flees from the people of Michoacán, who are such great archers?' But, after considering his options, Zuangua resolved on neutrality. 'Let the Mexica do their own killing,' he concluded; or, preferably, 'let the strangers kill the Mexica because, for many years, they have lived in the wrong way'. This attempt at diplomatic rapprochement represented the last chance for any prospect of Mesoamerican self-determination. Its failure effectively guaranteed Spanish hegemony. Again, the legacy of Mexica imperialism, and the enmity it had fostered, was ultimately self-defeating. The Triple Alliance would face its final challenge alone.

Cuitláhuac was formally invested as the tenth *huey tlatoani* on 16 September. He did not have much time to savour this achievement, for the Spaniards had unleashed an insidious new weapon against his dominion, one he was powerless to resist. The smallpox that devastated Cuba the previous year had now arrived in Mesoamerica. It tore indiscriminately through the indigenous communities; the impact on peoples who had no experience of, and no acquired immunity to, the disease can only be imagined. According to native accounts, the pandemic was introduced to Tenochtitlan in the Mexica 13th month (30 September–19 October), 'and lasted for 70 days, striking everywhere in the city and killing a vast number of our people'. Among the victims was Cuitláhuac, who died on 4 December, having ruled for only 80 days. He was far from alone. Amidst a great host of their subjects, great and small, Maxixcatl, Cortés' chief ally in Tlaxcala; the *tlatoani* of Tacuba, Chalco, and Cholula; and Zuangua, the *cazonci* of the Tarascans, all succumbed to this virulent, unprecedented plague.

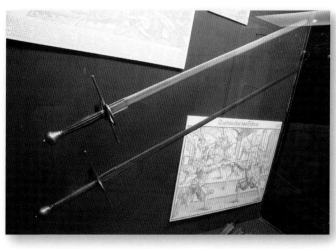

Several 16th-century swords, on display in the Palace of the Grand Master, Valletta, Malta. Generations of Eurasian military technological evolution – in composition, design, and application – had achieved their apotheosis in the swords borne by the Conquistadors. Whether wielded one or two handed, their reach and penetration endowed the Spaniards with two critical advantages in close-quarter combat. As Restall puts it: 'The one weapon, then, whose efficacy is indubitable was the steel sword. It alone was worth more than a horse, a gun, and a mastiff put together.' (Author's collection)

Diorama of the great marketplace of Tlatelolco. Provinces close to the capital contributed staple foodstuffs such as maize, beans, chia, and amaranth. From the north came maguey, honey, limes, chilies, and eagles; from the west, wood and salt; from the south, paper, cochineal, copal, tropical plumage, turquoise, greenstone, copper, cacao, seashells, and jaguar pelts; from the east, cotton, rubber, precious stones, and gold. (Museo Nacional de Antropologia, Mexico City – author's collection)

Spanish numbers, by contrast, were increasing, as ships continued to land at the coast. Some were intended as reinforcements for Narváez, others were expeditions in their own right, but their cargoes and crews (even Julián de Alderete, treasurer to King Charles V, who had been posted to the Indies to assert royal authority) all elected to join Cortés, swelling his numbers by 150 men and several precious horses. To the great delight of the *caudillo*, a final vessel arrived, commissioned by friends and family in Spain. It was laden with supplies, including harquebuses, gunpowder, crossbows, and crossbow bolts, as well as several more horses.

Cortés now moved to tighten the noose around Tenochtitlan. In December, he sent Sandoval north with 200 infantry, 12 crossbowmen and 20 cavalry to secure the road from Villa Rica to Tlaxcala by eliminating the Mexica garrisons at Zautla and Xalacingo. This accomplished, at the cost of only eight wounded, the detachment returned to Segura de la Frontera with a 'great spoil of women and boys' branded as slaves. With much greater significance, Cortés ordered Martin López to begin constructing a new fleet of brigantines at Tlaxcala. Cortés was gambling the advantages of building the vessels at this detached location – secrecy, security, plentiful on-site lumber and labour – would outweigh the subsequent challenge of transporting them across the mountains to Lake Texcoco. López drove his crews, and himself, tirelessly; one of his workers, Lázaro Guerrero, later said of his dedication to the brigantine project that 'he toiled in everything connected with their construction, all day long, and often, with the aid of candles, after dark and before dawn, working himself and directing and encouraging other workmen with the zeal of a man who comprehended the urgency of the matter'. López even resorted to damming the Zahuapan River during the dry season to form a small lake when he wanted to test whether the boats floated.

With all the component pieces of his campaign in place, Cortés concluded it was time to commence the final struggle in earnest. On 13 December, having posted Francisco de Orozco in command of a 60-man garrison, he marched out of Segura de la Frontera, making for Tlaxcala. It was there, on 28 December, he mustered his army for the return to Tenochtitlan. Thanks to the reinforcements that had arrived since *La Noche Triste*, he now had nine field guns, 40 horses, and 550 infantry, including 80 crossbowmen and harquebusiers. The rank and file he organized into nine companies of 60 men each, commanded by Alvarado, Olid, Sandoval, Gutierre de Badajoz, Francisco Verdugo, Rodríguez de Villafuerte, Pedro de Ircio, Andrés de Monjara, and Andrés de Tapia. Alongside the Spaniards marched 10,000 Tlaxcalteca under the command of Chichimecatecle, who had accepted baptism (as had Xicotencatl the Elder, now known to the Spaniards as Don Lorenzo de Vargas).

The Mexica could do little but await this onslaught. They had elected a new *huey tlatoani* – Cuauhtémoc, nephew to both Montezuma and Cuitláhuac and son of Ahuitzotl, the eighth *huey tlatoani* – but like his predecessor, he was content to remain on the defensive. This afforded several advantages. The Mexica were only too aware they could not withstand Spanish mobility in open country, but the tables would be turned once Cortés entered the Valley of Mexico. Here, Mexica canoes gave them the advantage of interior lines of communication, enabling them to strike at any point on the lake, while the Spaniards would be forced to march around it on foot. The Mexica would also be fighting close to their sources of supply, minimizing their own logistical burden while straining that of Cortés. And in the final analysis, the great metropolis of Tenochtitlan itself loomed as the ultimate weapon in the Mexica arsenal; its constricted urban environment was sure to exact a formidable toll in Conquistador blood.

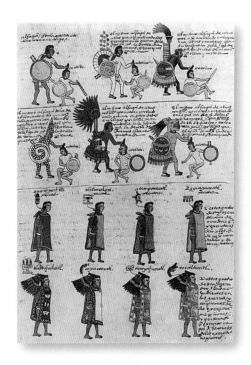

Mexica warriors, from the *Codex Mendoza*. In his account, the anonymous Conquistador writes: 'The armour they use in warfare are certain shirts like jupons, of quilted cotton the thickness of a finger and a half and sometimes two fingers, which is very strong. Over these they wear suits all of one piece and of a heavy cloth, which they tie in back; these are covered with feathers of different colours and look very jaunty. One company of soldiers will wear them in red and white, another in blue and yellow, and others in various ways. The lords wear certain smock-like coats which among us are of mail but theirs are of gold or gilt silver, and the strength of their feathered garments is proportionate to their weapons, so that they resist spears and arrows, and even the sword.' (Wikimedia Commons/Public domain)

Assuming it would be the least fortified, Cortés chose the highest and most difficult pass west out of Tlaxcala territory. Encountering minimal resistance, he entered the Valley of Mexico, smoke signals rising from the cities around the lake to herald his arrival. Settling down for the night of 29 December in Coatepec, a small-town tributary to Texcoco, Cortés was approached by the rebel warlord Ixtlilxochitl, who pledged his cooperation in the reduction of Tenochtitlan. An official delegation from Coanacochtzin received him the following day with offers of peace and hospitality. The Spaniards spent that night at Coatlinchan, only 8km from Texcoco. They entered the city on 31 December, only to find it deserted, the bulk of the population fleeing into the surrounding hills or, in a multitude of canoes, across the lake to Tenochtitlan, Coanacochtzin among them. Irked, Cortés sanctioned the standard chastisement for those cities that dared defy his authority; the unholy trinity of sack, slaughter, and slavery. In reality, he had little cause for complaint, given he had with minimal effort assumed control of the second city of the Triple Alliance. Its bountiful agricultural surpluses and secure site nearby the waterfront would serve him in good stead.

Eager to escape the fate of Texcoco, the local *tlaoani* began arriving at his court to offer their submission. Cortés was aware the Chalca cities south of the lake, reluctant tributaries to the Mexica, were eager to defect. The key to winning them over would be possession of Iztlapalapa, through which Tenochtitlan maintained its hegemony. Accordingly, having left about 350 Spaniards at Texcoco under Sandoval, Cortés set off with 200 men (including 18 cavalry, ten harquebusiers, and 30 crossbowmen) and up to 7,000 Allied warriors against that city.

At first, this sortie followed what to Cortés was becoming a familiar pattern. The Mexica drew up in loose order before Iztlapalapa, and covered the lake in canoes on his flank, but the Allied army was able to brush past what amounted to little more than harassment and occupy the city without any serious difficulty. In fact, however, Iztlapalapa was being used as bait, and Cortés had walked right into the trap. Having abandoned the city, the Mexica now made a breach in the Dyke of Netzahualcoyotl, which separated the salt water in the eastern section of the lake from the fresh water in the smaller, western portion of it. According to Díaz, 'so vast a flood of water rushed all of an instant into the town, that we must undoubtedly have all been drowned,' if the Texcoca serving with the Spaniards had not raised the alarm. As it was, many of the Tlaxcala, who were not accustomed to deep water, and consequently unable to swim, were lost. Even the Spaniards struggled with the elements; 'When I reached the water,' Cortés said, 'it was so deep and it flowed with such force that we had to leap across it'. The spoils looted during the sack of the city were lost, and the gunpowder, soaked, was useless. Finding what shelter they could, 'with our clothes completely drenched, with empty stomachs, and shivering with cold, we passed a most terrible night,' Díaz recalled. At dawn, the Mexica 'now came advancing towards us in vast numbers, both by land and water, and fell upon us'. Over the course of a fighting retreat, 'we lost two Spaniards and one horse, and great numbers of our men were wounded'. The Tlaxcala and Texcoca allies in the rearguard were especially roughly handled, many men never making it back to Texcoco. It was an embarrassing reverse, but it could have been a lot worse for Cortés, who had intended to overnight in Iztlapalapa. If the Mexica had waited until the cover of darkness to spring their gambit, they could have wiped out the entire invasion force in one stroke.

Despite this setback, ambassadors continued to arrive, pledging their allegiance to Cortés. When the key cities of Chalco and Tlamanalco petitioned for his support in eliminating their Mexica garrisons, Cortés dispatched Sandoval with a substantial force, which broke Tenochtitlan's grip over the region.

At the end of January, Martin López arrived with the brigantines from Tlaxcala, transported in their component pieces over the mountain passes by thousands of bearers. Work immediately commenced on assembling the vessels, which would be launched when a canal linking Texcoco to the shore was excavated. This would be time-consuming, but had Cortés established his shipyard on the lake itself, the Mexica could have sent thousands of canoes and seriously hindered, or possibly even halted, any progress. As it was, on three separate occasions during the construction phase, Mexica sorties had to be repelled from the shipyard even at its relatively secure inland site.

To keep the Mexica off balance, Cortés led Alvarado, Olid, 25 horse, 300 foot, six small field pieces, and a large number of Tlaxcala on another foray, this time around the northern perimeter of the lake. Xaltocan was stormed on 3 February, while Cuauhtitlan, Tenayucan, and Azcapotzalco, all of them abandoned, were subsequently occupied without resistance.

It was a different story when Cortés arrived at Tacuba on the landward side of Tenochtitlan's western-facing causeway, the route of the Spanish escape on *La Noche Triste*. The Mexica rallied to the defence of the city, the junior partner in the Triple Alliance, in significant numbers, and Cortés was only able to storm their fortified positions after considerable effort. When he sought to follow up this success by seizing the causeway, the Mexica drew him in until he was exposed, then committed their canoes on both his flanks. Cortés lost a number of men, and suffered more wounded, only extracting the survivors with difficulty. Several more days of cautious probing and verbal sparring followed before the Spaniards returned to Texcoco on 18 February. Cortés had confirmed his instincts in ordering construction of the brigantines were correct; without naval power to contest Mexica control of

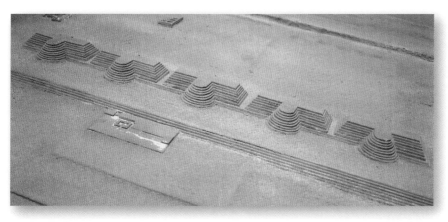

the lake, he could not secure the causeways, and without them, he could not invest Tenochtitlan.

There was good news from the coast, where more reinforcements had arrived from Hispaniola (three ships carrying 200 men, 60–70 horses, and stores of gunpowder, swords, crossbows, and harquebuses), and from Michoacán, where Cortés' ambassadors had been cordially received by Zincicha, the new *cazonci* of the Tarascans. But the Chalca cities to the south, subjected to Mexica raids, were pleading for assistance. The drawback to accepting the submission of these client states was having to guarantee their security. Cortés had to be aware that the more peoples who flocked to his banner, the more stretched he would be in defending them; a key imperative to ending the campaign quickly. But, until the brigantines were seaworthy, he would be forced to apply a reactive strategy. In March, Sandoval set out via Tlamanalco to Oaxtepec and Yecapixtla, routing the Mexica and their loyalists, and thwarting a major Mexica attempt to reclaim Chalco on 25 March. Cortés then decided to pacify the region once and for all. This time leaving Sandoval in charge at Texcoco, on 5 April he took Alvarado, Tapia, and Olid with 300 infantry, 30 cavalry, 20 crossbowmen, 15 harquebusiers, and more than 20,000 Texcoca–Tlaxcala allies, via Tlamanalco, Chalco, and Chimalhuacan against Cuernavaca in Xochimilca territory. Encountering a Mexica force occupying the rocky heights of Tlaycapan on 11 April, Cortés split his force and ordered multiple columns to converge after a direct assault straight up the steep slopes. The offensive was a costly failure (Cortés himself later admitted it was 'madness to attempt'), and the garrison only surrendered the following day because they had no access to water.

Cortés proceeded on to Oaxtepec, which capitulated without a fight. A large force of Mexica escaped from Yautepec only to be caught and wiped out at Xiutepec. Seizing Cuernavaca, bounded by its steep ravines, was more problematic. While Cortés led a frontal assault to pin the garrison in place, a detachment successfully outflanked the defence by clambering across the trees that spanned the gorge.

The positive outcome of this campaign secured the area south of the Valley of Mexico, inflicting fresh wounds to the prestige of the Triple Alliance, and further isolating Tenochtitlan from sources of supply and reinforcement.

Cortés marched back towards Lake Texcoco, on 16 April arriving at the city of Xochimilco, which was built on an island about half a kilometre from the southern shore. The Spaniards overwhelmed the defences, but in the evening Mexica reinforcements arrived from Tenochtitlan, seeking to trap the Conquistadors in the city by securing the causeway. Cortés led a charge of his cavalry to break their lines, but the Mexica had brought new weapons to the fight: makeshift polearms comprised of the enemy's own steel blades salvaged from *La Noche Triste* and fixed to wooden shafts. In the narrow space of the causeway, Díaz recorded, the Mexica 'received the charge of the cavalry with fixed lances, and wounded four of our horses'. Cortés' own mount 'fell down with its rider, and numbers of Mexicans instantly laid hold of our general, tore him away from the saddle, and were already carrying him off' when Cristóbal de Olea and some Tlaxcala 'flew to his assistance, and, by dint of heavy blows and good thrusts,' were able to cut him free. Olea received three very severe wounds for his efforts, but Cortés had again escaped the sacrificial knife. Several Spaniards were less lucky. Captured, they were sacrificed by Cuauhtémoc himself, their severed limbs being distributed throughout the empire as a warning to wavering tributaries they should remain loyal.

At dawn the next day, from atop the pyramid of Xochimilco, Cortés and his captains could see what they calculated to be 12,000 Mexica, in perhaps 1,000 canoes, paddling furiously towards them, their battle cries echoing across the lake. Another 10,000 warriors were on the march from Tenochtitlan. The Spaniards came under furious assault, both on land and by water. Cortés, aware he could not hold the city, ordered a retreat. Harassed all the way, the column briefly occupied Coyoacán on the return march to Texcoco.

Spanish cannon and harquebuses in action during the fight for Tenochtitlan, by Diego Rivera, Palacio Nacional, Mexico City. Artillery was critical to overcoming prepared Mexica defences. For example, when Cortés drove on the southern entrance to Tenochtitlan, he brought up two guns to open a path through a palisade wall. 'At the first shot, the wall fell to pieces; the shot broke through at the back,' Mexica accounts recorded. 'At the second, it collapsed to the ground. It was thrown down in various places, broken, torn open; the road was left clear.' (Author's collection)

It was then Cortés received the word he had been waiting for; the brigantines were ready, and on 28 April they were floated on Lake Texcoco. It was time to muster for the final assault. Cortés now had at his disposal 700 foot soldiers, 86 horsemen, and 118 harquebusiers and crossbowmen. His artillery comprised three heavy iron guns and 15 lighter field pieces. By this point, the number of available indigenous auxiliaries, their motivations ranging from revenge on the Mexica to opportunism or fear of Spanish reprisal, had swollen to the hundreds of thousands. The best fighters would serve on the front line, the rest performing rear echelon duties.

A *temalacatl*, Mexico City. Some captives, usually nobles and great warriors, were sacrificed in gladiatorial combat at the *temalacatl* during the feast of Tlacaxipehualizti. The body was taken to the captor's home, where it was eaten, the bones being displayed in the house as a sign of prestige. When Cortés broke into Tenochtitlan on 10 June 1521, he forced his way to the temple complex and set up a cannon on the *temalacatl* facing the Great Pyramid, giving it a clear field of fire across the plaza. When he was driven out of the city, Cortés had to abandon the cannon, which the Mexica dragged to the waterfront and tipped into the lake. (Author's collection)

Cortés organized his Spaniards into four divisions. He took personal command of the naval squadron that would crew the 13 brigantines, distributing 25 men, plus about six crossbowmen and harquebusiers per vessel. Ixtlilxochitl commanded a flotilla of his Texcoca in canoes that would serve as escorts.

The three divisions that were to invest Tenochtitlan by land were captained by Alvarado, Olid, and Sandoval, each assigned two precious cannon. Alvarado and Olid departed Texcoco on 22 May, marching around the northern shore of the lake to approach Tenochtitlan from the west. Sandoval would set out on 31 May, filing down the eastern flank of the lake to approach Tenochtitlan from the south.

Cortés sent Alvarado to Tacuba with 30 horsemen, 150 Spanish infantrymen, 18 crossbowmen and harquebusiers, and 50,000 indigenous warriors, primarily from Tlaxcala, Texcoco, Otumba, and Tolantzinco. The Tlaxcala were led by Chichimecatecle, while the Texcoca generals were Ixtlilxochitl's brother, Cuauhtliztactzin, and the lord of Chiautla, Chichinchiquatzin.

Olid accompanied Alvarado to Tacuba, then pressed further on to Coyoacán with 33 mounted Spaniards, 20 crossbowmen and harquebusiers, and 180 infantrymen. With him went 50,000 warriors from Tziuhcohuac and the other provinces to the north; their general was Tetlahuehuexquititzin, another brother of Ixtlilxochitl.

Sandoval was given command of 23 cavalrymen, 14 harquebusiers, 13 crossbowmen, and 170 infantrymen when he marched on Iztlapalapa. Accompanying him were the warriors from Chalco, Cuernavaca, and the other cities to the south, plus the Toltecs and Huexotzincans.

The fourth causeway, running north to Tepeyacac, was deliberately left open; Cortés was trying to tempt Cuauhtémoc into sortieing onto open ground, where Spanish mobility would count for a lot more than in the confined space of Tenochtitlan.

Cuauhtémoc refused to take the bait, but the Mexica did have to defend Chapultepec, the source of the aqueduct that brought fresh water to their city. Although the country was not ideal for cavalry, Alvarado and Olid were able to break the Mexica defence and seize this critical lifeline. For the next 75 days, the residents of Tenochtitlan would be forced to rely on whatever inadequate sources of water they could extract from wells and springs.

SPANISH BRIGANTINES ENGAGE MEXICA CANOES, LAKE TEXCOCO, 1 JUNE 1521 (PP. 76–77)

Cortés was aware he could not completely reduce Tenochtitlan without first wresting control of Lake Texcoco from Cuauhtémoc. To this end, he ordered brigantines constructed in Tlaxcala, then borne over the mountains piece by piece to be reassembled on the lakeshore. With his lieutenants already engaged in seizing the causeways that connected the Mexica capital to the mainland, Cortés judged the moment was right to lead his prefabricated armada into the fray (**1**). Paddling in the wake of the brigantines, the Conquistadors' allies, led by the chief Texcocan general Ixtlilxochitl, followed up in a flotilla of canoes (**2**).

Cortés was diverted from sailing straight to help Gonzalo de Sandoval at Iztlapalapa when he spotted many Mexica making smoke signals to Tenochtitlan from the small, high, and rocky island of Tepepolco about 5km offshore. Cortés landed 150 men, climbed the main hill, overwhelmed the fortifications, and killed all the defenders.

Having set off from the island, Cortés and his fleet encountered over 500 Mexica canoes filled with warriors (**3**). Many of the canoes had been upgraded to *chimalacalli* class, with additional heavy wooden shielding that offered the crews more protection (**4**). Undaunted, and with a strong breeze behind him, Cortés ordered the attack.

The other brigantines made swift progress, ramming or blasting their way through the Mexica canoes. The European vessels were too sturdy to be affected by Mexica missile weapons, and had too much sail and oar power to be grappled for boarding. Any Mexica canoes left behind by the brigantines were overwhelmed by the Texcoca canoes coming up in the rear of their Conquistador allies.

Ironically, the one Mexica success was Cortés' own flagship, which its captain, Rodríguez de Villafuerte (**5**), ran aground in the shallows (**6**). Seizing this opportunity, large numbers of Mexica promptly swarmed onboard (**7**). Villafuerte gave the order to abandon ship and fled to the rear of the vessel, ready to leap across to another brigantine coming up behind them, with Cortés at his side.

But Martín López (**8**), the man responsible for the construction and transportation of the brigantines, refused to give up so easily, and rallied the crew. They repelled the Mexica boarders, leaving the deck littered with dead and dying and slick with blood. Having observed a Mexica officer in feathers and plumes directing the assault from a nearby canoe, López has just killed him with a shot from a crossbow (**9**).

Mexica naval resistance was broken. As a confidant of Cortés later confirmed, 'This was a notable victory and was the key to that war, because we were now masters of the lake.' Isolated and besieged by land and water, Tenochtitlan, the beating heart of the Mexica Empire, was now doomed.

On 1 June, with his three subordinates in position at their respective causeways, Cortés initiated the naval component of the campaign. It was an immediate success, the brigantines smashing through a flotilla of Mexica canoes sent to intercept them. Cortés pressed on to seize the fortress of Xoloc on the main causeway from Iztlapalapa to Tenochtitlan, enabling Olid, his flanks covered by the brigantines, to link up with him there.

Having mobilized all available manpower, Cuauhtémoc divided his forces into four divisions; one to cover the northern causeway to Tepeyacac; a second to contest the Tacuba causeway with Alvarado; the third concentrated against Cortés, Olid, and Sandoval at Acachinanco; and a fourth held in reserve against any amphibious landing elsewhere in the city.

The battle for the causeways was now joined in earnest. Since the Mexica had not elected to break out of Tenochtitlan through Tepeyacac, but were using this unsecured avenue to bring in supplies, Cortés ordered Sandoval north from Iztlapalapa via Coyoacán and Tacuba to complete the blockade of the city. Taking 23 horse, 18 crossbowmen, about a hundred foot soldiers, and a contingent of allies, supported by three brigantines, Sandoval took up his new station.

After several days of indecisive fighting, Cortés took direct command of Olid's division on 10 June and personally led a major assault, giving orders to Alvarado and Sandoval to launch simultaneous attacks in their sectors. Using his brigantines as pontoons to bridge gaps in the causeway, Cortés overwhelmed the Mexica defences at the Eagle Gate, which marked the southern entrance to the city, and was able to advance as far as the Temple Complex. Sounding the alarm, the priests furiously beat the two-toned drum atop the Great Pyramid, its reverberations echoing over the din of combat, until the Spaniards scaled the heights and hurled them off the summit. More prosaically, Cortés took this opportunity to seize the mask of gold set with precious stones from the idol of Huitzilopochtli. Fighting raged all day; one Mexica, targeted by a Spanish horseman, was run through with his lance, but held on to it with his death grasp long enough for his comrades to swarm over the rider, drag him to the ground, and overwhelm him. When night fell, the Spaniards were finally forced to retreat, burning many

The Mexica, having dispossessed the Conquistadors of their Virgin Mary banner, rally to defend the Temple Complex in this scene from the *Codex Azcatitlan*. Drums were critical for Mexica command and control. Note the two styles on display here; the vertical *huehuetl* on the right, and the horizontal *teponaztli* on the left. (Wikimedia Commons/ Public domain)

buildings behind them as they fell back. Alvarado and Sandoval, in the west and north, made less progress, recalling their divisions while still 5–6km respectively from the centre of the city.

The brigantines, meanwhile, were keeping the Mexica under close blockade, intercepting those canoes stealing in and out of the city on supply runs. To send a clear signal to the people of Tenochtitlan that they were nowhere safe, a number of vessels were even able to fight their way up the canals and set fire to the Palace of Axayácatl. This was risky, however; the Mexica lined

their waterways with sharpened stakes to pinion the brigantines, snaring two and killing their commanders, Pedro Barba and Juan Portillo.

Cortés now resolved on a policy of total war. 'I saw how determined they were to die in their defence,' Cortés said of the Mexica; 'they gave us cause, and indeed obliged us, to destroy them utterly.' His allies (whose numbers increased every day, as warriors from ever more *altepetl* flocked to his banner, eager to be in on the kill) were following up each incremental gain made by the Spaniards, tearing down houses to remove them as platforms for the Mexica to launch missiles, using the rubble to fill in the canals and the breaches in the causeways so the next assault could penetrate deeper into the dying city. Tenochtitlan, a wonder of the world, was being torn apart stone by stone.

Satisfied he had the measure of the Mexica, from 15 June Cortés began making incursions into the city on a daily basis, varying his point of entry, but always fighting his way through to the temple complex before withdrawing, leaving carnage and destruction behind him. Some of his captains urged him to advance his headquarters into Tenochtitlan, but the *caudillo*, cautious about losing control of the causeways and being trapped – again – inside the metropolis, insisted on overnighting in Xoloc.

From 20 June, Cortés began probing west after occupying the Temple Complex, looking to link up with Alvarado. His subordinate, however, was not making much progress along the Tacuba Causeway. Frustrated, Alvarado allowed himself to be drawn into a trap. On 23 June, the vanguard of his division was lured into Tlatelolco by a feigned withdrawal across a narrow breach in the causeway, and then ambushed by overwhelming numbers of Mexica. With the breach they had crossed now blocked by hundreds of canoes, the Spaniards were routed into a deeper channel as they desperately sought a way out of the city. Dozens of them were left floundering, easy prey; the Mexica killed many outright, dragging others off to be sacrificed.

Despite this success, the siege was going badly for the Mexica. Casualties were high, much of the city was in ruins, and even with strict rationing of the food and available water, famine was beginning to grip the population. Sensing weakness, formerly subordinate peoples continued defecting. It must have particularly stung, Alonso de Aguilar commented, when 'the lord who ruled Xochimilco came over to our side, because his people, with their canoes, fought most cruelly against the Mexicans and contributed largely to their destruction'. Internal divisions, too, threatened the façade of Mexica unity. When two sons of Moctezuma II, Axayaca and Xoxopehualoc, proposed opening negotiations with Cortés, Cuauhtémoc had them executed. In reprisal, their followers killed the high priests of Huitzilopochtli and Tezcatlipoca. Under pressure within as well as without, and unable to hold the

Diego Rivera, in this segment from his murals in the Palacio Nacional, Mexico City, emphasizes the relentless nature of the Conquistadors in their pursuit of ultimate victory. Despite no previous experience of warfare on European terms, the Mexica made them fight for every inch of ground. In order to counter the Spanish horsemen, for example, 'we dredged each canal, made it wider, made it deeper, made its sides steeper,' their accounts record. 'Everywhere we made the canals as difficult and dangerous as possible. On the roads we built ramparts, barricades. We made the passages between houses as difficult as possible.' (Author's collection)

entire perimeter of the city, Cuauhtémoc withdrew his forces into Tlatelolco.

Seeking to exploit this advantage, Cortés ordered another coordinated assault by all of his divisions, which were to convene at the great marketplace in Tlatelolco. Leaving his cavalry to screen the Tepeyacac Causeway, Sandoval linked up with Alvarado at Tacuba. Supported by half a dozen brigantines and 3,000 Allied war canoes, this combined force would drive on Tlatelolco from the west. After entering the city from the south, Cortés would split his command into three columns, which would separately force the roads leading from Tenochtitlan to Tlatelolco. Cortés himself would lead 100 Spaniards, Tapia would captain another 80, while Alderete, the king's treasurer, was assigned 70. All three detachments were supported by eight horsemen and tens of thousands of Allied warriors, sappers, and bearers. At dawn on Sunday, 30 June, having heard mass, Cortés ordered the assault he hoped would end the conflict in one decisive stroke.

At first, all went well. In the account of Ixtlilxochitl, the allies fought their way into Tlatelolco, 'killing many and taking houses, bridges and fortifications without sparing anyone, in such a way that it seemed that they would take Mexico that day'. But then the balance tipped. Mexica resistance stiffened as the allies advanced deeper into irregular and unfamiliar city blocks. The columns stalled, and then began to fall back. Retreat became a rout when word spread the Mexica had succeeded in opening a gap in one of the roads behind Alderete's column; it was just too wide to leap over, and the water in the breach was too deep to ford. 'When they realized what was happening, they acted just like drunk men,' the Mexica recounted, describing the Spaniards launching themselves into the breach in a desperate bid to swim to safety. While some Mexica dogged their heels with missile fire, others arrived in swarms of canoes: 'We overtook them; we slew or captured them in abundance.'

An Eagle warrior bust. In Mexica cosmology, those who died in battle went to *ilhuicac*, the place of the sun, as did those who were captured in battle and later sacrificed. After four years in *ilhuicac*, they returned to the Earth in the forms of birds and butterflies. (Museo Nacional de Antropologia, Mexico City – author's collection)

Alerted that a complete collapse was in progress, Cortés galloped to the scene, dismounted, and began hauling individual soldiers out of the chaos. 'The enemy attacked so fiercely that in attempting to kill the Spaniards they leapt into the water after them,' as he described it. Then some of those warriors seized him. Again, his life was there for the taking. But the Mexica obsession with capturing their nemesis and not killing him on the spot once more proved their undoing. Cristóbal de Olea and Ixtlilxochitl swooped in and cut the *caudillo* free, hacking the arms off several Mexica in the process, buying time for more Spaniards, including Antonio de Quiñones, to join in the rescue. Cortés was pulled clear, but Olea was left behind and finally overwhelmed.

Cortés wanted to make a stand, but Quiñones, shouting to be heard above the shrieks and war cries of the exultant Mexica, warned him against it: 'Let us go and at least save your own person, for you know that if you are killed, we are all lost.' Cortés, reluctantly, saw reason, and ordered anyone still alive to pull out of the city and back to the relative safety of Xoloc. The triumphant Mexica decapitated the heads of the slain Spaniards and tossed

Replica of a Jaguar Knight helmet. 'To defend the head they wear things like heads of serpents, or tigers, or lions or wolves,' an anonymous Conquistador recorded of the Mexica warrior elite, 'and the man's head lies inside the animal's jaws as though it were devouring him'. (Museo del Ejército y Fuerza Aérea, Mexico City – author's collection)

them at the feet of Alvarado and Sandoval, taunting them with the news that their *caudillo* was dead, and they were next. Demoralized, the two captains withdrew back to their camps on the Tacuba and Tepeyacac causeways.

Cortés, in fact, still lived, but dozens of Spaniards along with a cannon, a brigantine, and eight precious horses had been lost in the disaster, along with a multitude of allies. Succumbing to a fate worse than death, dozens more Spaniards were captured alive, including Cristóbal de Guzmán, Cortés' major-domo, who had been with him from the beginning. That evening the survivors, nursing their wounds, could only watch as their comrades were dragged, naked, up the steep slopes of the Great Pyramid of Tlatelolco. Listening to the screams as Conquistador hearts were torn, still beating, from their breasts, 'we greatly desired to put a stop to this,' Cortés lamented, but, 'we were unable to do so'.

It was the greatest victory for the Mexica since *La Noche Triste*. Intoxicated by this success, the next morning the Mexica at last went over onto the offensive, launching wave after wave of assaults on each of the Spanish camps. Cuauhtémoc was active on the diplomatic front too, sending messengers to the *tlatoani* of key cities throughout the Valley of Mexico with gruesome trophies; the flayed heads of the sacrificial victims, as well as their hands and feet, and the heads of several horses too. And indeed, Cortés' allies suddenly melted away. Most of the warriors from Cholula, Huexotzinco, Texcoco, Chalco, Tlalmanalco, even Tlaxcala, slunk home, leaving only token forces with the Spaniards.

Compounding his burdens, envoys from cities that had accepted his suzerainty began arriving at Xoloc, pleading with Cortés for protection from the tribes and polities stirred up against them by Mexica propaganda. It was the supreme crisis of the campaign. Had Cortés elected to conserve his strength and insist that his client states fend for themselves, they may have elected to reach some accommodation with Cuauhtémoc instead. The tables would then turn completely; the Spaniards would have found themselves besieged by the Mexica, cut off from resupply or reinforcement from, or escape to, the coast.

Cortés rose to the challenge; 'although our defeat was so recent and we needed help more than we could give it,' he later explained, 'I determined to go to their aid'. He dispatched Tapia south with 80 foot soldiers and ten horsemen to the aid of Cuernavaca, which was under attack by highland barbarians from Malinalco and Huitzuco, and Sandoval with 100 infantry and 18 horsemen to the border of Tlaxcala, where Toluca was threatened by its neighbours, Matlaltzinca and Malinalco.

This intervention was a high-stakes gamble; its success proved decisive. Complete victory in both campaigns stabilized the diplomatic situation and proved the Spaniards had lost none of their prowess in battle. The Allied contingents that had so mysteriously vanished just days earlier now flocked to reenlist under Cortés. With their tactical and logistical support, he could resume his systematic reduction of Tenochtitlan.

This 1899 painting entitled 'The Last Days of Tenochtitlan' by William de Leftwich Dodge captures the bleak horror of the city's death throes. When the Conquistadors eliminated the final pockets of resistance, they found the few survivors huddled in such deprivation that 'it was beyond our understanding how they could endure it,' Bernal Díaz recalled; 'we came across piles of dead and were forced to walk over them'. (Wikimedia Commons/Public domain)

By this point, too, it was evident the Mexica had shot their bolt. Not only did the attacks on the Conquistador camps tail off, the defence of the city was clearly faltering. Every night, for weeks, the Mexica had laboured to excavate gaps in the causeways, repair their walls, and erect new barricades in the streets. Now they lacked the energy to do so. Mexica accounts describe people reduced to eating lizards, corncobs, weeds, leather, even dirt; 'Nothing can compare with the horrors of that siege and the agonies of the starving.' Then Alvarado's division reached, and destroyed, the last fresh water spring remaining to the city's inhabitants, leaving them no alternative to drinking the highly brackish lake water, many dying of dysentery as a direct result. So few warriors remained fit to bear arms that Cuauhtémoc was conscripting women in a desperate bid to keep an army in the field. According to Aguilar, when the Spaniards 'began killing them and saw they were women, there was dismay on both sides'.

Bolstered by the timely arrival of more ships at Villa Rica, bearing fresh manpower and, even more important, fresh supplies of gunpowder, Cortés initiated a new phase of unrelenting pressure. Mexica resistance began to collapse in the face of Allied incursions swarming through the streets and the constant bombardment from the brigantines stationed offshore. Another turning point was reached when Ixtlilxochitl captured his brother, Coanacochtzin. The loyalist Texcoca, fighting alongside the Mexica, now defected to Cortés. This was a body blow to Cuauhtémoc, who at this point lost any hope of aid arriving from outside Tenochtitlan.

The fighting was now becoming very one-sided. The Spanish sprang an ambush, using their cavalry to lure the beleaguered Mexica into a trap in which more than 600 were killed. Perhaps more significant, at least another 2,000 laid down their arms rather than throw their lives away in what was becoming an ever more pointless struggle.

The Great Temple of Tlatelolco. This city, somewhere between a suburb and a satellite of Tenochtitlan, had been forcibly incorporated within the Triple Alliance in 1473, its last *tlatoani* hurling himself off the Great Temple when he saw that defeat was inevitable. It always retained its distinctive identity, however. Ironically, the Mexica were to make their last stand here in 1521, symbolized by the effigy of Huitzilopochtli being removed from the Templo Mayor in Tenochtitlan to Tlatelolco. When Cortés saw smoke rising from the summit of the Great Temple on 25 July 1521, he knew the last Mexica defensive line had been broken. (Author's collection)

Note: the illustration covers a base area of 5.7km x 4.7km

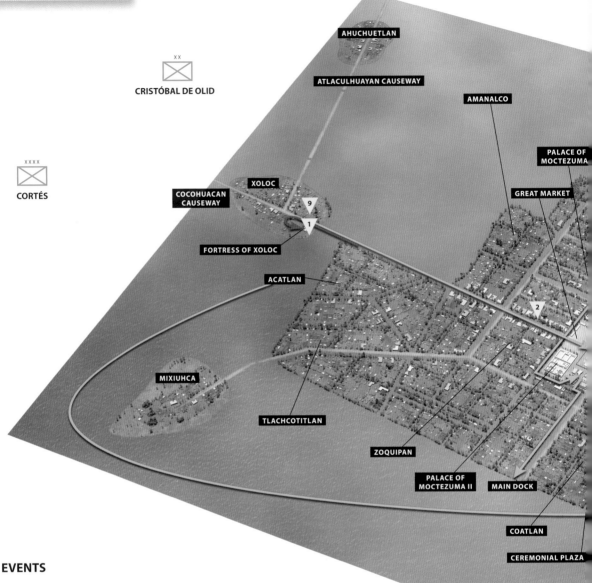

MEXICA
1. Between 50,000 and 75,000 warriors.

CRISTÓBAL DE OLID

CORTÉS

AHUCHUETLAN
ATLACULHUAYAN CAUSEWAY
AMANALCO
PALACE OF MOCTEZUMA
XOLOC
COCOHUACAN CAUSEWAY
GREAT MARKET
FORTRESS OF XOLOC
ACATLAN
MIXIUHCA
TLACHCOTITLAN
ZOQUIPAN
PALACE OF MOCTEZUMA II
MAIN DOCK
COATLAN
CEREMONIAL PLAZA

▼ EVENTS

1. 1 June 1521: Cortés establishes his headquarters in the fortress of Xoloc.

2. 10 June 1521: Cortés breaches the southern gate and advances as far as the Temple Complex before being driven out of the city.

3. Mid-June, 1521: the brigantines are able to fight their way through the canals into the heart of Tenochtitlan, burning the Palace of Axayácatl on their way into the city, and the Royal Aviary on their way out.

4. 15 June 1521: Cortés begins making daily incursions into the city, reaching the Temple Complex before withdrawing.

5. 20 June 1521: from this date, Cortés begins probing west from the Temple Complex, seeking to link up with Alvarado.

6. 23 June 1521: Alvarado is lured into a Mexica ambush in Tlatelolco, and forced to retreat after suffering heavy losses.

7. Late June, 1521: Cuauhtémoc withdraws into Tlatelolco.

8. 30 June 1521: Cortés orders a general assault. While Alvarado and Sandoval advance from the west, Cortés drives into the city from the south, splitting his division into three columns. When the Mexica counterattack at a breach in a causeway, the assault breaks down and is routed.

9. Early July, 1521: emboldened by this success, Cuauhtémoc seizes the initiative, laying siege to the Allied encampments. Deserted by most of his native auxiliaries and having further diluted his surviving Conquistadors by diverting detachments to the aid of those potentates still loyal in the surrounding regions, Cortés can do little more than hang on grimly.

10. 21 July 1521: with Mexica strength waning, Cortés swings back over to the offensive. Allied spearheads clear the entire road to Tacuba, linking the western and southern divisions; the Palace of Cuauhtémoc is burned.

11. 25 July 1521: the Allied offensive seizes the great market in Tlatelolco; all three Allied divisions are now united.

12. 12 August 1521: Allied offensive shatters the final Mexica defensive line.

13. 13 August 1521: Cuauhtémoc, the last *huey tlatoani*, is captured while trying to escape by canoe. He surrenders Tenochtitlan to Cortés. This event signals the end of the Mexica Empire.

THE FALL OF TENOCHTITLAN, JUNE–AUGUST 1521

Having secured control of Lake Texcoco, Cortés and his allies advance into Tenochtitlan from the causeways to the mainland from the south, west, and north. Despite fierce resistance led by Cuauhtémoc, the city eventually falls, bringing the Mexica Empire to an end.

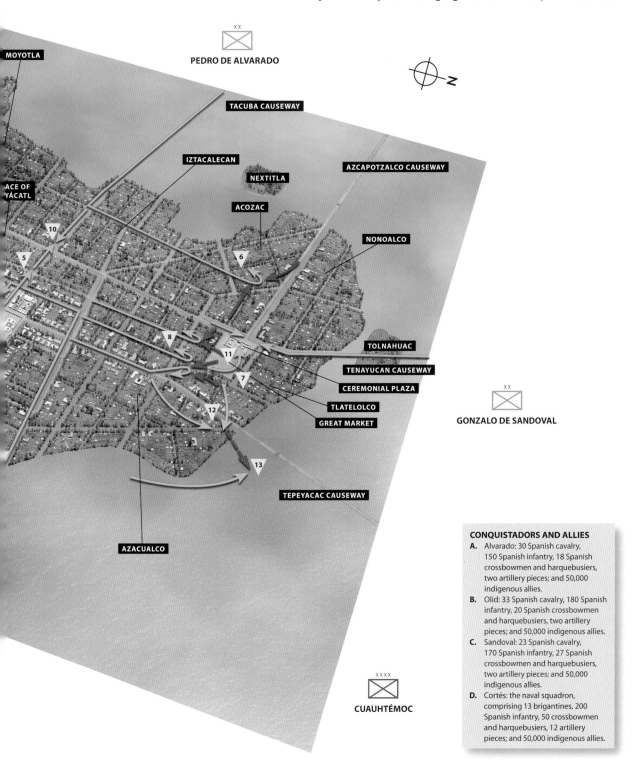

MOYOTLA

PEDRO DE ALVARADO

TACUBA CAUSEWAY

IZTACALECAN

NEXTITLA

AZCAPOTZALCO CAUSEWAY

ACE OF YÁCATL

ACOZAC

NONOALCO

10

5

6

8

11

TOLNAHUAC

7

TENAYUCAN CAUSEWAY

CEREMONIAL PLAZA

12

TLATELOLCO

GREAT MARKET

GONZALO DE SANDOVAL

13

TEPEYACAC CAUSEWAY

AZACUALCO

CUAUHTÉMOC

CONQUISTADORS AND ALLIES

A. Alvarado: 30 Spanish cavalry, 150 Spanish infantry, 18 Spanish crossbowmen and harquebusiers, two artillery pieces; and 50,000 indigenous allies.

B. Olid: 33 Spanish cavalry, 180 Spanish infantry, 20 Spanish crossbowmen and harquebusiers, two artillery pieces; and 50,000 indigenous allies.

C. Sandoval: 23 Spanish cavalry, 170 Spanish infantry, 27 Spanish crossbowmen and harquebusiers, two artillery pieces; and 50,000 indigenous allies.

D. Cortés: the naval squadron, comprising 13 brigantines, 200 Spanish infantry, 50 crossbowmen and harquebusiers, 12 artillery pieces; and 50,000 indigenous allies.

The surrender of Cuauhtémoc, last *huey tlatoani* of the Mexica, to Cortés. Note Cuauhtémoc has his hand on Cortés' dagger, which he begged the conqueror to draw and end his shame with. (Author's collection)

On 21 July, Allied spearheads cleared the entire road to Tacuba, linking their columns. That same day, the Palace of Cuauhtémoc was burned. On 25 July, all three Allied divisions advanced to the great marketplace in Tlatelolco, where Cuauhtémoc had elected to make a last stand. Overcoming desperate resistance, four horsemen broke in and were able to gallop around its perimeter, lancing defenders at will. Then the Great Pyramid was stormed, the temple at its summit burned, and Cortés' banner placed in its stead. The following day, the *caudillo* himself was able to climb to this elevation, from which he could confirm seventh-eighths of the city was now in his hands.

Cortés finally established his headquarters in the city proper, on the roof of a house in the Amaxac district. Here, in his tent with its crimson canopy, he awaited word of Cuauhtémoc's surrender. Given he had by now, in his own account, killed 'an infinite number of the enemy, we each day expected them to sue for peace'. But still the *huey tlatoani* equivocated. His stalling bought him only a few days respite. On 12 August, Cortés resumed hostilities. By now, the indigenous allies of the Spaniards could not be restrained, and what was left of the Mexica, packed into the shrunken pocket of the city they still possessed, could no longer act in self-defence. 'No one could go anywhere,' their account laments; 'We jostled and crowded against one another. Many, in fact, died trampled in the press.' Tens of thousands of helpless men, women, and children were slaughtered in an orgy of bloodletting that shocked even the Conquistadors.

This fresco from the Government Palace, entitled 'Victory of the people of Tlaxcala', emphasizes the numbers, and motivation, of the allied contingents who enlisted for the final campaign against the Triple Alliance. The ancient enmity between them and the Mexica spilled over into atrocity. Cortés' chaplain, Father López de Gómara, attributed much of the death toll in Tenochtitlan over the last, desperate days of the siege in 1521 to 'our Indian friends, who would spare the life of no Mexican, no matter how they were reprimanded for it'. Even Cortés professed to be shocked; 'no race has ever practised such fierce and unnatural cruelty,' he claimed, as the allies he himself had unleashed on the city. (Scala/Art Resource, NY)

The following day, Tlacotzin, the *cihuacoatl*, approached Cortés with a final statement from Cuauhtémoc; the *huey tlatoani* preferred death to surrender. Coldly, the *caudillo* replied that if so, all the Mexica would die alongside him. Cortés then gave orders for Alvarado to drive the last remnant of the population to the waterfront, where Sandoval would be waiting for them with the brigantines. But for all their defiance, there was no fight left in the Mexica. The allies, above all the Tlaxcala, had neither pity nor mercy for what remained of their old adversaries. They again ran amok, and 'There was not one man among us whose heart did not bleed at the sound of these killings,' Cortés later confessed. A general exodus then occurred as all of its inhabitants who still had the strength to do so fled Tenochtitlan, leaving behind houses crammed with dead bodies, 'and among them several poor people were found still alive, though too weak to stand, and lying in their own filth,' according to Diaz. The beautiful city that had greeted Cortés two years earlier was now a wasteland that 'looked as if it had been ploughed up, for the famished inhabitants had dug up every root out of the ground, and had even peeled the bark from the trees, to still their hunger'.

The final cost in human lives will never be known for certain. Cortés' chaplain, Father López de Gómara, calculated the Mexica death toll at 100,000, 'not including those who died from hunger and disease'. The *Florentine Codex* lists an even higher figure, over 240,000. By comparison, the Spaniards probably lost somewhere in the range of 100 men over the three months of the final siege – a startling disparity, and a testament to the high quality of Conquistador tactical doctrine, coupled with Eurasian technology, horses, and pathogens. But even with those odds stacked against them, the Mexica proved a remorseless adversary. It should be borne in mind that nearly 1,000 Spaniards had been killed out of the approximately 1,800 in all who campaigned in Mesoamerica between 1519 and 1521. And even in its death throes, Tenochtitlan took a fearsome toll of Cortés' allies; more than 30,000 Texcoca alone perished while playing their part in subduing the Triple Alliance, according to Ixtlilxochitl.

Even at the end, some high-ranking Mexica still sought to escape Tenochtitlan by canoe across the lake. Among them was Cuauhtémoc. He and his entourage (including Tetlepanquetzatzin, the *tlatoani* of Tacuba) were intercepted by a brigantine captained by García Holguín and brought before Cortés, to whom the last *huey tlatoani* formally surrendered. At that moment, silence fell over Tenochtitlan, and the Mexica Empire of the Triple Alliance ceased to exist. It was 13 August, the day of St Hippolytus, patron saint of horses.

This memorial to Cuauhtémoc stands in Tlatelolco, where the Mexica made their last stand. The inscription reads: 'On 13 August 1521 / heroically defended by Cuauhtémoc / Tlatelolco fell to the power of Hernan Cortés / This was neither triumph nor defeat / But the painful birth of the mestizo people who are Mexico today'. (Author's collection)

The global strategic situation, 1530

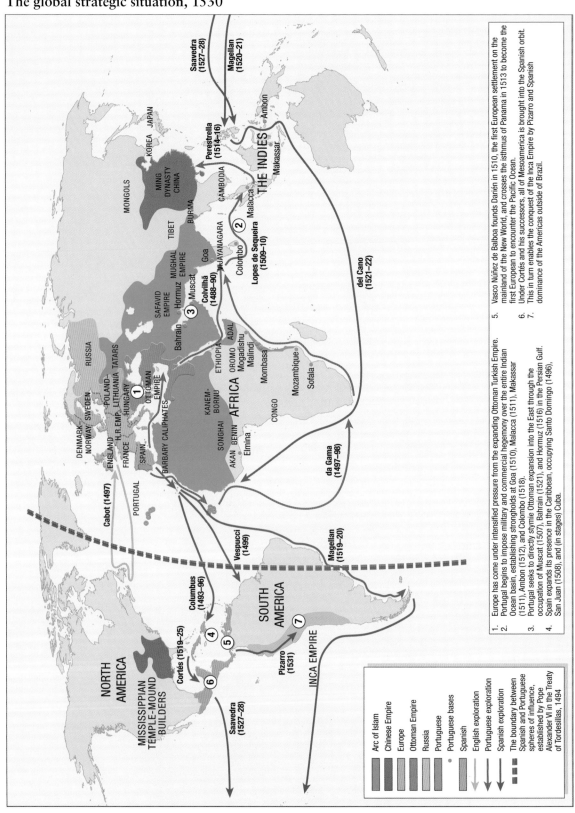

1. Europe has come under intensified pressure from the expanding Ottoman Turkish Empire.
2. Portugal begins to impose military and commercial hegemony over the entire Indian Ocean basin, establishing strongholds at Goa (1510), Malacca (1511), Makassar (1511), Ambon (1512), and Colombo (1518).
3. Portugal seeks to directly stymie Ottoman expansion into the East through the occupation of Muscat (1507), Bahrain (1521), and Hormuz (1516) in the Persian Gulf.
4. Spain expands its presence in the Caribbean, occupying Santo Domingo (1496), San Juan (1508), and (in stages) Cuba.
5. Vasco Núñez de Balboa founds Darién in 1510, the first European settlement on the mainland of the New World, and crosses the isthmus of Panama in 1513 to become the first European to encounter the Pacific Ocean.
6. Under Cortés and his successors, all of Mesoamerica is brought into the Spanish orbit.
7. This in turn enables the conquest of the Inca Empire by Pizarro and Spanish dominance of the Americas outside of Brazil.

88

AFTERMATH

The most striking feature of the new order was its continuity. The Spaniards kept the networks of tribute and exchange as established by the Mexica functionally intact, only with themselves now inserted at the apex of the system. That remnant of the Mexica nobility considered potential threats to the new regime was liquidated, either by being hanged or thrown alive to the dogs, the latter including both the *tlacatecatl* (military commander) and the *tlillancalqui* (Keeper of the House of Darkness) of Tenochtitlan. But on a city-by-city basis, most *tlatoani* remained in office, the only effective difference being they now answered to foreign overlords who required them to adopt the Christian faith in place of their own.

As a gesture of reconciliation, Cuauhtémoc was formally installed as ruler of Tenochtitlan to oversee reconstruction of the ruined city. The fact he amounted to nothing more than a figurehead was brutally brought home when he could not account for the gold that had disappeared on *La Noche Triste*. In a bid to extract the truth, he was tortured by being tied to a pole and having his feet dipped in oil, which were then set alight.

Much to their frustration, even interrogatory practices of this nature failed to add much to what the Conquistadors had already looted, which amounted to, at most, 200,000 pesos in value. After deducting the royal fifth of 37,000 pesos, Cortés then took 29,600 pesos as his fifth of the rest. The total available for distribution was, therefore, a little less than 120,000 pesos. After bonus payments to the senior captains were distributed, the cavalry in the expedition received 80 pesos each; crossbowmen, harquebusiers, and other special forces 50–60 pesos each; while the rank and file had to make do with even less. This barely covered the purchase of the tools of the trade – a sword cost 50 pesos, a crossbow 60 – scant reward given the extent of the dangers and the significance of the victory.

Cortés had two alternatives at his disposal to compensate his disgruntled erstwhile comrades in arms for their lack of financial remuneration. Those who wanted to put their campaigning days behind them were granted *encomiendas*, and settled down as the new plantation aristocracy.

El suplicio de Cuauhtémoc [The Torture of Cuauhtémoc] by Leandro Izaguirre (1892). Cortés had the last huey tlatoani of Tenochtitlan, along with Tetlepanquetzatzin, the tlatoani of Tacuba, tortured in order to extract the last ounce of gold from the defeated empire. When Tetlepanquetzatzin looked at Cuauhtémoc for a sign he should confess anything in order to end their agony, the proud young Mexica only derided him for his weakness and asked, 'Do you think I, then, am taking pleasure in my bath?' Cuauhtémoc survived, but he walked with a limp for the rest of his life. (Museo Nacional de Arte, Mexico City/Wikimedia Commons/Public domain)

The monument to Mexica resistance, at the intersection of Avenida de los Insurgentes and Paseo de la Reforma in Mexico City. The inscription at the base reads: 'In memory of Quautemoc [sic] and the warriors who fought heroically in defence of their homeland'. (Alejandro Linares Garcia/Wikimedia Commons/CC-BY-SA-3.0)

The apotheosis of Hernan Cortés; a contemporary illustration by Weiditz Trachtenbuch. Among the coats of arms depicted on the shield, note his own in the lower right quadrant, granted by Charles V in 1525. It incorporates the black two-headed eagle of the Holy Roman Empire; a golden lion on a red field symbolizing the personal qualities Cortés applied to consummating the conquest; three crowns representing the three Mexica *huey tlatoani* – Moctezuma II, Cuitláhuac, and Cuauhtémoc – overcome by Cortés; and a depiction of Tenochtitlan. Encircling these are symbols of the seven city-states around Lake Texcoco and their lords that Cortés defeated, with the grant specifying they be 'shown as prisoners bound with a chain'. (Wikimedia Commons/ Public domain)

Those who still burned with the Conquistador spirit were assigned new territories to subdue in the name of Charles V and the expanding frontiers of New Spain. Sandoval was dispatched south with an expedition to Tustepec before moving on to Coatzacoalco. Francisco de Orozco was ordered into Oaxaca. Diego de Pineda and Vicente López went to conquer Pánuco. Olid set off for the independent kingdom of Michoacán, where he accepted the abject surrender of the *cazonci* in Tzintzuntzan, then pushed further west into Colliman. Alvarado pacified Tututepec and Tehuantepec.

The fortunes of these later enterprises were mixed. Olid was executed in 1525 after leading a rebellion in a bid to carve out an empire of his own in the New World. Narváez, released from prison in Mexico, returned to Spain, where he was appointed *Adelantado* (governor) of Florida by Charles V. But his 1528 expedition to locate the Fountain of Youth was a total failure that cost him his life and that of all but four other participants. Alvarado rose to become the first governor of Guatemala before being killed in 1541 leading from the front during a campaign in Guadalajara.

Cortés himself campaigned in 1522 to the east against the Huaxtecs of Pánuco. The following year, confirmation arrived from Madrid that he had been named Captain-General and Governor of New Spain. This long-sought legitimacy marked the pinnacle of his career. But in 1526, he finally pushed his luck too far when he led an expedition to Honduras. In his absence, factional infighting and imperial bureaucratic interference had undermined his authority. In a bid to restore his good name, he set off for Spain in 1528. Charles V appointed him Marquis of the Valley of Oaxaca, granted him a twelfth part of the profits of all his conquests, and gifted him with an *encomienda* of 23,000 vassals, making him one of the richest

men in the Spanish Empire. Cortés returned to New Spain in 1530, but he was soon made aware his economic security did not translate to political influence. The empire needed administration, not heroics, and the era of the Conquistador was already drawing to a close. Cortés remained actively involved in exploring the Pacific Ocean and the Gulf of Mexico, but, bedevilled by creditors and lawsuits, he departed New Spain once more in 1540 to again plead his case in Madrid. By this time, the magic of his name had worn off, and he was dismissed at court as a relic of the past. He would die in his native country without ever returning to the New World that he had delivered to an emperor who now turned his back on him.

Far from benefiting by their association with Cortés, his native allies ultimately found themselves having exchanged the threat of subordination to Tenochtitlan for the reality of subordination to Madrid. Even the Tlaxcala, who returned home, burdened with loot, and with the satisfaction of having exacted revenge upon the Mexica for generations of enforced isolation, soon found themselves even more effectively marginalized by their ostensible partners. The Spaniards, who had no desire to foster the rise of a powerful new empire astride their supply lines to the coast, failed to comply with the terms of their agreement whereby they would aid Tlaxcala in imposing regional hegemony. The Tlaxcala retained a measure of autonomy, but in the end the greatest friends of the Conquistadors were as fully subsumed within the Spanish imperial project as their ancestral enemies.

In the final analysis, the only real winners to emerge from the Conquest were the Spanish crown and the Catholic Church, who now had a secure base on the American mainland from which they could expand their presence in the New World, both secular and divine.

What did it all mean? For nigh on 500 years, the context of the Conquest has been seized upon to justify a succession of ideological perspectives on history. None of these stand up to any real scrutiny.

In the traditional narrative, the Conquistador triumph emphasized the inherent intellectual, technological, and moral superiority of Western culture, legitimizing the process of European imperialism that unfolded globally over the ensuing four centuries. Certainly, Cortés and his cohorts lost no opportunity to justify their actions as being in the long-term interests of the peoples they had subjugated. It was they who introduced Christianity, the wheel, and a whole new suite of flora and fauna that fundamentally enriched the lives of those they ruled over. Of course, asserting the superiority of the colonial project in Mesoamerica meant denigrating the indigenous value system it had supplanted. This process began by highlighting the practice of institutionalized mass human sacrifice as representing the definitive quality of Mesoamerican culture as opposed to being merely one aspect of it. True, every year thousands of human beings ended their lives bent backwards over an altar atop a Mexica pyramid, their hearts offered to the pitiless gods. This unquestionably represented the most poisonous organized religion in human history, and the world is a better place without it. But to its practitioners, this ritual sacrifice was necessary in order to preserve the harmony of the universe. The Roman Empire butchered as many people on an annual basis in its arenas for no reason other than its entertainment value, and the Renaissance

The final resting place of Hernan Cortés is located here in the church of Jesús Nazareno e Inmaculada Concepción, Mexico City. In death, his body endured a saga almost as contested as it had during his life. In his will, Cortés asked to be buried in a monastery built to his order in Coyoacán, Mexico. His wishes were ignored and he was buried two days later in the mausoleum of the Duke of Medina in the monastery of San Isidoro del Campo in Seville, Spain. Three years later, his body was moved to the altar of Santa Catarina in the same place. Six years later, in 1556, his body was finally taken to Mexico to be buried in the church of San Francisco de Texcoco. In 1629, when Don Pedro Cortés, the fourth Marqués del Valle (and the last male descendant of Cortés) died, the viceroy of New Spain decided to exhume the remains, which spent nine years in the palace before being reburied in the *sagrario* (side chapel) of a Franciscan church, where they spent the next 156 years. However, in 1794, his bones were moved to the Hospital de Jesús Nazareno, which he had founded. With passions running high after Mexico's War of Independence, in 1823 the statue and the coat of arms of Cortés were sent to Palermo in Sicily while the bones were hidden. About 13 years later, the remains were reburied behind a wall at the adjacent Jesús Nazareno e Inmaculada Concepción church, where they were rediscovered on 24 November 1946. (Author's collection)

The Hospital de Jesús Nazareno in Mexico City. Built on the orders of Cortés during the reconstruction of Tenochtitlan to serve the indigenous Mexica, it has been a functioning medical facility since 1524, making it one of the oldest continuously occupied buildings in Mexico City. (Diego Delso, delso.photo, License CC-BY-SA)

The aftermath of the Conquest from the Mexica point of view; dispossession and slavery, as depicted by Diego Rivera, Palacio Nacional, Mexico City. One Conquistador was quite open about what he and his compatriots hoped they would accomplish in the New World: 'to serve God and his Majesty, to give light to those who were in the darkness, and to grow rich as all men desire to do'. (Author's collection)

Europe of the Conquistadors prided itself on inheriting the cultural legacy of the Caesars without debating its legitimacy. Furthermore, given the contemporary record of the Catholic Church in Europe, with the Papacy's militant campaigns of forced conversion, ethnic cleansing, and physical annihilation against those minorities (Jews, Muslims) and apostates (Cathars, Hussites) trapped within its orbit, the arrival of the Inquisition and the auto-da-fé in the New World was a mixed blessing at best.

Conversely, the fall of Tenochtitlan was not a case study in the desecration of an Edenic indigenous culture by the colonialist West, as asserted by contemporary revisionist narratives. The Mexica in 1519 were not childlike innocents but citizens of a mature and sophisticated civilization. The elite of their society were warriors, administrators, and priests whose overriding priority was the political and economic security of their empire. They struggled to fit the strangers at the gate into their world as they knew it, but they approached the problem rationally within the established cultural traditions of Mesoamerica.

Their fatal flaw was the underlying nature of the imperial system itself. The tributary states at the periphery of the empire maintained their own distinct identities and were only very loosely integrated into the political core. The sole guarantor of compliance was Mexica prowess at war, which necessitated military campaigning by the Triple Alliance on an annual basis in order to emphasize the futility of resistance (the notorious mass human sacrifices of prisoners taken during these seasonal campaigns were therefore as much political propaganda as religious piety). The problem with this model of administration was threefold.

First, this system was efficient in that it minimized the burden of direct administration from Tenochtitlan by farming it out to subordinated local elites. But this depended on the absence of a rival great power around which these disaffected elites could unite. The Mexica were correct in their assumption that no such entity existed within Mesoamerica. They could never have anticipated this vacancy would be filled by the Spaniards from outside it. The intervention of Cortés therefore served as the catalyst – not the instrument – for the collapse of Mexica hegemony.

Second, even in the absence of such destabilization, sooner or later the Triple Alliance would have bumped up against the geopolitical constraints that afflicted all of pre-Columbian America. The empire was a machine geared for war, but its very success in pushing the frontier ever outward meant the logistics of supporting such campaigns were being stretched to breaking point.

In a land with no navigable rivers and no beasts of burden, there had to be a limit beyond which the Mexica could no longer project power (the fact the empire of their contemporaries in South America, the Inca, was orders of magnitude larger despite being no more sophisticated in terms of political organization or technology was owed to the existence of the llama, a beast of burden unavailable in Mesoamerica). If the empire could no longer expand, it could no longer maintain the steady flow of tribute and prestige inward to Tenochtitlan that rationalized its existence.

The true legacy of Cortés to the peoples of Mexico, according to Diego Rivera, Palacio Nacional, Mexico City. Note the branding of slaves at the left side of this scene, and the burning of indigenous writings on the right. The loss of this cultural heritage was even more damaging than the physical degradation. 'In their time, therefore, great strictness was observed in the ceremonies to their gods, but now they feel neither fear nor shame,' Father Alonso de Aguilar lamented: 'now that they are Christians, and as though in retribution for our sins, most of them come to church by force, and with very little fear and reverence; they gossip and talk, and walk out during the principal part of the Mass and the sermon.' (Author's collection)

Third, even if it could survive this challenge to its underlying ethos, the empire would have been doomed sooner or later by the boom and bust population cycle that defined the fitful course of civilization in Mesoamerica. Again and again, the centralization of power in a singular political polity would encourage urbanization, economic specialization and a spike in population, which would lead in turn to excessive stress on the environment. Inevitably, a tipping point would be reached. The land could no longer meet the needs of the inhabitants, and the polity could not compensate by drawing on resources from other regions because of the lack of navigable rivers and beasts of burden by which to distribute them. With their basic subsistence needs not being satisfied, the populace would lose faith in the political hierarchy of the polity. Insurrection and disintegration would follow.

In his account of the Conquest written many years after the events he witnessed, Díaz still struggled to express the awe he felt in first laying eyes on the glory of Tenochtitlan: 'It was all so wonderful that I do not know how to describe this first glimpse of things never heard of, seen, or dreamed of before.' But this metropolis was living on borrowed time. Had European intervention been delayed until a later generation, their only evidence the Mexica ever existed would have been abandoned pyramids and legends of mighty gods and warriors. This was the fate of Teotihuacan, the once great city that had been the centre of the Mesoamerican universe in its own time. Tenochtitlan was trapped in the same web of fate.

In the final analysis, for all his ambition, opportunism, and tactical genius, it wasn't Cortés who delivered Mesoamerica to European imperial authority; Eurasian diseases did that. Even if the first Spaniards in the New World had arrived in the spirit of true Christian charity, the pathogens they bore with them would still have effectively annihilated every community, every culture they touched. It was the same story everywhere in the Americas; as Massachusetts Governor John Winthrop put it, 'For the natives, they are neare all dead of small poxe, so as the Lord hathe cleared our title to what we possess.' And that was only the first wave; the initial pandemic was followed by measles, and typhus, and influenza, until the demographic collapse was complete. This was neither intended nor desired by the conquerors

Monumento al Mestizaje, by Julián Martínez y M. Maldonado (1982). This group, commissioned by Mexican President López Portillo, represents Hernan Cortés (modelled on the Mexican actor of Spanish origin Germán Robles), La Malinche, and their son, Martín Cortés. Reflecting Mexico's conflicted interpretations of its past, the arrangement was originally placed in the centre of Coyoacán, near the site of Cortés' country house, but it was moved to the less prominent Jardín Xicoténcatl in the Barrio de San Diego, Churubusco, in response to public protests. Even so, the figure of the child later disappeared, presumably abducted. (Javier Delgado Rosas/Wikimedia Commons/CC-BY-SA-3.0)

themselves; the aristocrats were mortified by the loss of labour to work the fields, the clerics by the loss of souls to save. But it happened; and with or without the Conquistadors, the New World would have been depopulated and exposed to exploitation by a weapon more powerful and more absolute than anything else they brought with them from Europe.

So, what does the fate of the Mexica teach us? To return to the theme of extra-terrestrial invasion with which we began our account, perhaps the most important lesson to be drawn from the Conquest is how easily the innate human quality of seizing on near-term solutions without considering the long-term consequences can be exploited. 'In our obsession with antagonisms of the moment, we often forget how much unites all the members of humanity,' US President Ronald Reagan once mused in an address to the United Nations General Assembly; 'Perhaps we need some outside, universal threat to make us recognize this common bond. I occasionally think how quickly our differences worldwide would vanish if we were facing an alien threat from outside this world.' If the fate of the Mexica is any guide, this perspective is fatally flawed. Such a threat need not follow the template established by H. G. Wells, and visualized by a host of (inferior) cinematic successors, whereby an alien armada descends on our planet and commences indiscriminately liquidating the human population. The easier path would be to follow the example of Cortés; identify the dominant indigenous imperial power, spearhead a coalition against it, then use the established beachhead as a portal for subsequent colonization and exploitation. If this scenario ever does play out, perhaps someday our descendants will pause to consider how completely their world was subjugated and transformed culturally and biologically, and wonder, too, how they let it happen.

BIBLIOGRAPHY

Primary sources

Cortés, Hernán, *Letters from Mexico*, New Haven: Yale University Press, 2001

de Fuentes, Patricia, *The Conquistadors: First-Person Accounts of the Conquest of Mexico*, New York: Orion Press, 1963

de Gómara, Francisco López, *Cortés: The Life of the Conqueror*, Berkeley: University of California Press, 1964

de Sahagún, Bernardino, *We People Here: Nahuatl Accounts of the Conquest of Mexico*, Berkeley: University of California Press, 1993

del Castillo, Bernal Díaz, *The Conquest of New Spain*, Baltimore: Penguin Books, 1963

Portilla, Miguel León, *The Broken Spears: The Aztec Account of the Conquest of Mexico*, Boston: Beacon Press, 1962

Schwartz, Stuart B. (ed.), *Victors and Vanquished: Spanish and Nahua Views of the Conquest of Mexico*, Boston: Bedford/St Martins, 2000

General works on the Mexica

Carrasco, David, *City of Sacrifice: The Aztec Empire and the Role of Violence in Civilization*, Boston: Beacon Press, 1999

Clendinnen, Inga, *The Cost of Courage in Aztec Society: Essays on Mesoamerican Society and Culture*, New York: Cambridge University Press, 2010

de Rojas, José Luis, *Tenochtitlan: Capital of the Aztec Empire*, Gainesville: University Press of Florida, 2012

Isaac, Barry L., 'Aztec Warfare: Goals and Battlefield Comportment', *Ethnology*, Vol. 22, No. 2, 1983, pp. 121–31

Mundy, Barbara E., *The Death of Aztec Tenochtitlan, the Life of Mexico City*, Austin: University of Texas Press, 2015

Pohl, John M. D., *Aztec, Mixtec and Zapotec Armies* (Men-at-Arms 239), Oxford: Osprey Publishing, 1991

——, *Aztec Warrior AD 1325–1521* (Warrior 32), Oxford, Osprey Publishing, 2001

General works on the Conquistadors

Pohl, John M. D., *The Conquistador 1492–1550* (Warrior 40), Oxford, Osprey Publishing, 2001

Wise, Terence, *The Conquistadores* (Men-at-Arms 101), Oxford, Osprey Publishing, 1980

Wood, Michael, *Conquistadors*, Berkeley: University of California Press, 2000

Works on the campaign

Berdan, Frances et al. (eds.), *Aztec Imperial Strategies*, Washington, DC: Dumbarton Oaks Research Library and Collection, 1996

Brooks, Francis J., 'Motecuzoma Xocoyotl, Hernán Cortés, and Bernal Díaz del Castillo: The Construction of an Arrest', *The Hispanic American Historical Review*, Vol. 75, No. 2, 1995, pp. 149–83

Chaliand, Gérard, *Mirrors of a Disaster, The Spanish Military Conquest of America*, New Brunswick: Transaction Publishers, 2005

Clendinnen, Inga, '"Fierce and Unnatural Cruelty": Cortés and the Conquest of Mexico', *Representations*, No. 33, Winter, 1991, pp. 65–100

Daniel, Douglas A., 'Tactical Factors in the Spanish Conquest of the Aztecs', *Anthropological Quarterly*, Vol. 65, No. 4, October 1992, pp. 187–94

Hassig, Ross, *Aztec Warfare, Imperial Expansion and Political Control*, Norman: University of Oklahoma Press, 1995

——, *Mexico and the Spanish Conquest*, Norman: University of Oklahoma Press, 2006

Kerner, Alex, 'Espionage and Field Intelligence in the Conquest of México, 1519–1521', *Journal of Military History*, Vol. 78, No. 2, April 2014, pp. 469–501

Levy, Buddy, *Conquistador: Hernán Cortés, King Montezuma, and the Last Stand of the Aztecs*, New York: Bantam Books, 2008

Manzanilla, Linda, and Luján, Leónardo López, *Atlas Histórico de Mesoamérica*, México City: Larousse, 2003

Martin, Scott, 'Command Decisions: The Conquest of Mexico and the Friedman-Savage Utility Function', *Social Science History*, Vol. 34, No. 4, Winter 2010, pp. 499–522

Marks, Richard Lee, *Cortés: The Great Adventurer and the Fate of Aztec Mexico*, New York: A. Knopf, 1993

Matthew, Laura E., and Oudijk, Michael R. (eds.), *Indian Conquistadors: Indigenous Allies in the Conquest of Mesoamerica*, Norman: University of Oklahoma Press, 2007

McEwan, Colin, and Luján, Leónardo López (eds.), *Moctezuma: Aztec Ruler*, London: British Museum, 2009

Restall, Matthew, *Seven Myths of the Spanish Conquest*, New York: Oxford University Press, 2003

——, 'The New Conquest History', *History Compass*, Vol. 10, No. 2, 2012, pp. 60–151

Thomas, Hugh, *Conquest: Montezuma, Cortés, and the Fall of Old Mexico*, New York: Simon & Schuster, 1993

Todorov, Tzvetan, *The Conquest of America: The Question of the Other*, New York: Harper Perennial, 1996

Townsend, Camilla, 'Burying the White Gods: New Perspectives on the Conquest of Mexico', *The American Historical Review*, Vol. 108, No. 3, June 2003, pp. 659–87

——, *Malintzins' Choices: An Indian Woman in the Conquest of Mexico*, Albuquerque: University of New Mexico Press, 2006

White, Jon Manchip, *Cortés and the Downfall of the Aztec Empire: A Study in a Conflict of Cultures*, New York: St Martin's Press, 1971

INDEX

References to images are in **bold**.